Today Someone I Love Passed Away

Written by
Dianne Ahern

Illustrated by
William Shurtliff

Published by Aunt Dee's Attic

Today Someone I Love Passed Away
© 2008 Aunt Dee's Attic

A Book from
AUNT DEE'S ATTIC

Published by
Aunt Dee's Attic
415 Detroit Street, Suite 200
Ann Arbor, MI 48104

Printed and bound in Italy

Nihil Obstat:	Msgr. Robert Lunsford
	Censor Librorum
Imprimatur:	Most Reverend Carl F. Mengeling
	Bishop of Lansing
	February 2007

The *Nihil Obstat* and *Imprimatur* are the official declarations that a book or pamphlet is free of doctrinal or moral error. No implication is contained therein that those who have granted the Nihil Obstat and Imprimatur agree with the contents, opinions, or statements expressed.

Library of Congress Control Number: 2007908259

ISBN 0-9679437-4-4

1   2   3   4   5   6   7   8   9   10

First Edition

www.auntdeesattic.com

Dedication

This book is dedicated to those special people in my life who passed away this year: my sister, confidante, and lifelong friend, Barbara; my best friend, Joanne; my good friend Lyn; and my treasured zia, Isabella. God be with you, my friends.

❧

Acknowledgments

A very special thank you to all the people who helped make this book possible, especially. . .

. . . Father Jeffrey Njus, Pastor of Saint Thomas the Apostle Catholic Church, Ann Arbor, Michigan, who directs our attention to the saving power of Jesus' sacrifice on the Cross, and for his love and fervor for the job of shepherding us all toward heaven;

. . . Josiah Shurtiliff, for his able assistance, review, and comment, and especially for doing the research into the funeral customs and traditions of other religions;

. . . those good friends who read early drafts of this book and provided comments and advice, especially Leo DiGiulio, Lisa Tucci, Emily Shurtliff, Sandra Snabb, and Shiobhan Kelly;

. . . LeAnn Fields, copy editor par excellence;

. . . Jillian Downey, for the text design and composition;

. . . and those who lent their likenesses to make the story come to light in the illustrations, including Timothy and Sheri Marotz and their children Christian, Zachary and Meghan, Ronald Driessche, Josiah and Emily Shurtliff and their daughter Evelyn, Sandra Snabb, Reverend Fr. Jeffrey Njus, Reverend Fr. Timothy Krzyzaniak, William Vida Shurtliff and his son Isaiah, Gregory and Keenan Allion, and the Muehlig Funeral Chapel, Inc.

Grandpa's Coming to Stay

"It's just not fair!" yelled Danny. "I'm always the one who has to give up things. You promised that when we moved into this new house that Ted and I would each have our own room. I'm not moving in with Ted. You can't make me!"

Danny's father, Mr. Walsh, tried to explain. "I'm sorry, but it just has to happen. Your grandpa has been living alone since Grandma passed away two years ago and he isn't doing very well. He needs to live with us now," he said to Danny. "He's our family."

"But he can have Ted's room, or Ella's room! Why does he have to take my room?" pleaded Danny.

"Because your room is close to a bathroom. That will become Grandpa's bathroom, and you and Ted will have to share with Ella," said his father.

"We have to give up our bathroom, too! This just isn't fair. I hate you!" shouted Danny as he ran outside, slamming the door behind him.

"Well, that didn't go over so well, did it?" Mrs. Walsh sighed. "I knew Danny would be disappointed, but I didn't think he would be that upset," she said to her husband.

Danny was the middle of three children, with Theodore (Ted, as he preferred being called) the oldest and Ella, who had just turned five, the youngest. Danny always seemed the least selfish of the kids, but he was also the one who was the most excited to have his own room when they moved into the new house. He was also excited about having it decorated so it resembled a gigantic aquarium. The walls were painted deep blue with murals of fish of all sizes, colorful coral reefs, weird sea creatures, and a sunken ship. When he asked to have a real aquarium in his room, his parents agreed, with the stipulation that he promise to take care of it all by himself. From the start he had been very responsible in taking care of the fish and the other crawly things in the aquarium.

"Well, Ted, it looks like you're going to have to be the 'big brother' and make Danny understand that your room is his room too," said their mother.

"Oh, sure," said Ted, looking disgusted. "Like I want to share my room with that little busybody. I don't want him messing with my stuff!"

Just then Mr. Walsh broke into the conversation. "There will be no name-calling. You have your stuff, just like Danny has his stuff. But you two will share

a room and you will get along. It is no longer your room; it belongs to you and Danny. Understand?" said his father sternly.

Their five-year-old sister watched and listened intently. She didn't want her big brothers messing up her room or her bathroom, but before she could protest, she felt her father's eyes on her.

"Don't you say a word, Miss Ella!" (Whenever he calls her "Miss Ella" she knows that he is really serious.) "You are all going to share and you are all going to love having your grandpa live with us. You just wait and see!" insisted their father.

The Walsh family spent the next week preparing for Grandpa's arrival. Danny's parents weren't wasting any time in getting his room ready for Grandpa. Danny stood in the doorway and watched as his parents applied one, then two coats of paint over his sea world. It made him feel like a part of him was being taken away. He was so sad.

Danny moved out of sight to listen to his parents talking while they painted. He learned that all of Grandpa's possessions were coming with him to this house. Grandpa's bed and dresser, his favorite chair, and television supposedly would fit nicely in Danny's room. Whatever possessions didn't fit in the room would be stored in the attic for the time being. Danny's aquarium would have to be moved out of the bedroom and put at the end of the upstairs hallway, just outside the boys' room, where Danny could still take care of it.

To cheer Danny up, his parents offered to redecorate Ted's room, if the boys could both agree on a theme. Ted loved all sports, including water sports. Danny, of course, loved the sea and fish. As a compromise, they decided that one side of the room would have sailing and surfboarding scenes for Ted, and the other side would have a beach and an ocean with a scuba diver surrounded by fishes, lobsters, and octopi. Although they would rather choke than admit it, both boys loved working together on their new room.

Fish Stories

Grandpa Vernon's moving day was a sunny Sunday in early spring. He had lived by himself for over two years since his wife died, and it had become quite lonely for him. He was looking forward to being part of a busy family again.

Grandpa Vernon noticed that Danny was not at all friendly toward him at first. He suspected it had something to do with the room assignments, but he wasn't absolutely sure. "When the time is right, I'll do something special for Danny," Grandpa Vernon thought to himself.

The next Saturday, as Grandpa was getting ready to go downstairs for lunch, he noticed Danny sitting by the aquarium in the hallway with his nose smashed up against the glass. He turned to ask Danny what he was looking at, stooping down to look into the aquarium with him.

"My fish and my sunken treasure," mumbled Danny. "I'm pretending that I'm in the middle of the ocean, far away from this house. I wish I were old enough to join the Navy or a deep sea exploration team or something like that," pouted Danny.

"You don't say! Danny, did you know that I was a blue water sailor?" asked Grandpa Vernon.

"Oh yeah?" said Danny sarcastically. "So what's a blue water sailor and where's your boat? How come I have never seen it?"

"I sold the boat a few years ago, after we found out that your grandma was sick. You were probably too young to remember it. But your grandmother and I actually sailed around the world together in our boat. Blue water sailing is the term they use for open ocean sailing."

Danny peeled his smashed nose away from the aquarium and stared at his grandpa in great disbelief. "You and Grandma? You actually sailed around the world?"

"That's right. And what adventures we had. My, oh, my! It seems sailing's either in your blood or it isn't."

"You know," continued Grandpa, "my ancestors (your ancestors, too), are from the Isle of Man—that's an island in the middle of the Irish Sea. The sea was our ancestors' life. They fished for a living and sailed for recreation. In fact, you have a cousin who still lives on the Isle of Man where he owns and operates a commercial fishing business.

"There's sea on your grandmother's side of the family too. She grew up in a fishing village on the southern coast of France. Why, she learned to skipper

a boat before she learned to ride a two-wheeler," declared Grandpa. "The way you love that aquarium, I'd say you have some of that 'sea blood' running through your veins, too."

"Would you tell me about your sailing adventures sometime?" asked Danny.

"Yes, of course," said Grandpa, "I would really like that. My old globe of the world is in the attic with my other things," he said, pointing to the ceiling. "Maybe after lunch, I can show you some of the places we sailed. I have ever so many stories to tell you."

"Hey! That's a deal," said Danny excitedly. He was so anxious to hear stories about sailing and the ocean that he almost forgot he was mad about Grandpa taking his bedroom.

After lunch, Danny and Grandpa climbed the stairs to the attic, a huge room that covered nearly the entire second story of the house. There were big round windows at each end that let in lots of light. The windows were etched with arches and circles, and looked kind of like the stained glass windows in churches but with clear glass. Sometimes the sun coming through the windows would make rainbows that decorated the walls and floor.

On one side of the attic, Danny's mother had arranged three big chests—one for him, one for Ted, and one for Ella. In them she would store stuff like pictures they painted, their First Reconciliation and First Communion books, report cards, and other weird keepsakes like their first tooth. She said that someday they'll be glad she saved all that stuff.

On the other side of the attic, Danny's dad had put Grandpa Vernon's things, including old furniture, two huge trunks, a full-length mirror, and a great big old globe of the world. These were surrounded by boxes full of what looked like old people's junk, thought Danny.

Together they pulled the globe free, then pulled out a dusty old stuffed chair for Grandpa and a small stool for Danny and placed them by one of the windows so they could have good light. Just then Ella and Ted joined them. Curiosity had gotten the best of them.

"This globe is really old," laughed Grandpa. "Look at the names of these countries. So many have changed."

"What good is an old globe?" complained Danny.

"Oh, they will probably keep changing the names of places for as long as we live, and then some. That's politics. But what doesn't change are the oceans! This globe will do just fine for showing you where your grandma and I sailed," said Grandpa Vernon.

First Lady

Grandpa Vernon spent the next two hours telling stories about how he and his wife sailed around the world on their boat, First Lady. They began at the Isle of Man, and from there to England, then down the Mediterranean coast of Europe, all around the Greek Islands, and even through the Indian Ocean and the South China Sea. They had sailed in the South Pacific, and even crossed the Atlantic Ocean twice. Once they encountered pirates looking for fuel—but since a sailboat doesn't need much fuel, the pirates were disappointed. More than once they ran across fierce, hurricane-like storms, big freighters that nearly ran them over, and curious island natives who had never before met English-speaking people.

Danny just could not believe it. His grandparents were real adventurers. For the first time, he was really glad that his grandpa was HIS GRANDPA! He began to get a really proud feeling in his chest.

Where Is Heaven?

The trips to the attic with Grandpa soon became a regular event in the Walsh household. For weeks Danny, and now Ted and Ella, had been going up to the attic with him after lunch—just the four of them. Some days Grandpa would tell them stories of his sailing adventures; some days they read books together; other days they would read from the Bible and discuss their favorite Bible stories. Every once in a while they would go up there just to be together and talk about what was on their minds. Today was one of those days.

"What's this?" asked Ella, as she snatched a white veil out of one of Grandpa Vernon's trunks. She placed the veil on her head and began to dance around.

"That was the veil your grandmother wore on our wedding day," explained Grandpa Vernon. "I wondered what happened to it! Do you like it, Ella? Maybe someday your mother will fix it up so you can wear it on your wedding day!"

"Oh, Grandpa. It's so pretty." Ella swayed back and forth as she admired the way she looked in the long mirror. In the reflection, she could see her grandpa looking at her—he was smiling, and she smiled back at him. Their eyes twinkled.

"Where did Grandma go?" asked Ella.

"Well, you were just a toddler when it happened. Your grandma had been sick for a very long time and she passed away about two years ago. You probably don't remember her, but the boys do. I like to think that she is in heaven now."

"Does it make you sad to talk about her?" asked Ted.

"Maybe sometimes," replied Grandpa. "But then I think about all the good and happy times we had together—we had a full life—and because of that, I cannot be sad. Besides, she so wanted to go to heaven and see Jesus—that was her final prayer. If I think about her being in heaven now—with all the angels and saints—well, I just cannot be sad."

"Where's heaven?" asked a confused Ella.

"That's where God lives. It's a place full of angels and saints," explained Danny. "I think it is up in the sky somewhere. Ms. Kelly told us that we can get to heaven, and by the time we get there, we'll be perfect—we'll be saints, too."

"What's heaven like?" asked Ella, as she crawled up on Grandpa's lap still wearing her grandma's bridal veil.

"It's a place so wonderful and so complete that no matter how much you loved the people back on earth, you have no desire and no need to return to earth to be with them," explained Grandpa.

"You know, when your grandma was sick, she told me that she dreamed of going to heaven and seeing Jesus. She would read the Gospel of John where it says:

"Do not let your hearts be troubled. You have faith in God; have faith also in me. In my father's house there are many dwelling places. If there were not, would I have told you that I am going to prepare a place for you? And if I prepare a place for you, I will come back again and take you there myself, so that where I am you also may be." (John 14:1–3)

"Then she would tell me just what she expected heaven to be like. She imagined that all those 'dwelling places' that Jesus talked about in John's Gospel would be like an endless array of different rooms in heaven. She believed that once you were in heaven you could visit all or any of the rooms whenever you wished. Each of the rooms could be as big as the whole world and each would have a separate door.

"She imagined one door would open into a music room where she could go and listen to beautiful music for as long as she wanted—concerts and operas, and everything musical. She even expected that in that heavenly room she could sing with a beautiful voice, although she could never carry a tune here on earth. "Another room would be a walking room where she could explore woods, or forests, or Rome, or Paris, or wherever she wanted. She imagined that in this room she could walk forever and her legs would never get tired.

"Quite often she would talk of 'the sailing room' in heaven, where there would be perfect winds and perfect weather and, once I joined her in heaven, we could happily sail off into a sunset.

"One of her favorite places to imagine was the 'family room' where she would be reunited with her parents and grandparents and where other members of the family would be welcomed as each of them reached heaven."

The four of them sat quietly, thinking about heaven for a while.

"Ted, what do you think heaven is like?" asked Grandpa Vernon, breaking the silence.

"I think it'll be a place where there is nothing but peace, just peace. There won't be any fighting or bad things happening ever. And there won't be any homework or chores—no arguments or anger or stress. You know—just peace," replied Ted.

"How about you, little Ella, what do you think heaven will be like?" asked Grandpa.

"I think it will be like being up here with you, Grandpa. When we are all in heaven, you can tell us stories forever and ever!" exclaimed Ella.

The four of them laughed and then talked some more. Grandpa let Ella dig deeper in the trunk, until she found Grandma's wedding dress, a beautiful gown made of fine embroidered silk. The skirt had layers and layers of underskirts, called crinolines, that made the dress poof out like a bell. Ella buried herself in the crinolines and giggled with glee.

Grandpa watched his granddaughter for a while, sighed and then said, "Children, I am a little tired. I think I need to rest a bit before dinner. We can come back up here later in the week."

The boys straightened up their attic getaway and helped Ella put away Grandma's wedding dress and veil. As they followed Grandpa downstairs, Danny noticed that the elderly man was moving more slowly and seemed more tired than usual. It also seemed to him that it was getting harder for Grandpa to get in and out of chairs.

What's a Soul?

Danny, Ted, and Ella had just arrived home from school and were hungry. Their mom always had a snack ready for them when they got home. Today when they came in the door she had a serious look on her face.

"Children, I have some sad news. You know Christina, your little friend from next door who's been sick and in the hospital? Her mother called me this afternoon and told me that she had passed away."

"What does 'passed away' mean?" asked Ella. "Grandpa said that Grandma 'passed away'—what does that mean?"

"It means that a person has passed from the hands of those who love and care for them here on earth into the loving hands of God," said their mother.

"Oh," said Ella, not really understanding, but not ready to ask another question, either.

"Let's say a prayer that her soul is on its way to heaven and pray that God will provide comfort for her family," said their mother.

They held hands around the kitchen table, and said the *Hail Mary* and *Our Father* prayers together out loud. At the end, Danny's mother said a prayer he had not heard before. "May Christina's soul and the souls of all the faithful departed through the mercy of God rest in peace. Amen."

Suddenly Danny's heart felt very heavy. He felt the color go out of his face and his eyes began to sting around the corners. Their neighbor and playmate Christina was just a little girl—only a year older than Ella. Before Christina got sick, she and Ella would play dolls together almost every day. He used to tease the girls, and Christina would pretend to get mad at him—but she really didn't. It was just their way of kidding around with each other. Christina was a really nice little girl. Now Christina was dead—he was old enough to know that 'passed away' was another way of saying that she had died. How could that be?

"Momma, why would God let someone like Christina die? It doesn't seem fair," protested Danny. He was becoming angry.

"Oh, Danny, it is so hard to understand. I don't know why God let her die. No one can know. It may be that God wanted her to be with Him in heaven more than He wanted her here on earth with us. Perhaps God saw her soul was so pure right now that He decided to spare her from all the difficulties and temptations that go along with growing up. Perhaps He didn't want her to be in pain or to struggle with any more illnesses. We don't know why, but what we do know is that it is God's will and we have to accept it," said Danny's mother, in a very loving voice.

"You mean, God's will, like in the *Our Father* when we say, 'Thy will be done on earth as it is in heaven?'" questioned Danny.

"That's exactly it," replied Danny's mother. "You can bet that if it were my will, or if you were making the decisions, nobody we love would ever die. The world would be a pretty crowded place if God left it up to us. But He doesn't.

"Christina's visitation is planned for Thursday afternoon and evening, and her Funeral Mass will be on Friday. We will go as a family. Your dad will be taking time off work. You should all plan on wearing your good clothes and dress shoes."

She then put out glasses of milk along with crackers and peanut butter for their after-school snack. But none of them felt like eating.

Later that day, Grandpa Vernon found the children sitting quietly in the attic. He had learned about Christina's death and felt like he needed to spend some time with his grandchildren. Mostly, he wanted to be around to answer

any questions they might have. Danny and Ted's eyes looked a little red, probably from crying. Little Ella just looked confused.

"What happens when someone passes away?" questioned Ella as she plopped down on the stool in front of Grandpa's big stuffed chair. She decided she wanted answers and Grandpa Vernon always had good ones.

"In a technical sense, when a person dies or passes away, the person's heart stops beating and he or she stops breathing," explained Grandpa Vernon. "A person who has died cannot be awakened, and he or she cannot live on earth any longer. However, a person who has stopped breathing will live on forever in heaven, or possibly in hell, if they've turned away from God."

The children's faces showed surprise at hearing the word "hell." Their parents forbid them from using that word, particularly in everyday conversation. But the way that Grandpa Vernon used it seemed okay.

"Something very special happens when someone dies—something very extraordinary," said Grandpa Vernon in a mysterious, whispering voice. The children leaned in to listen.

"When a person breathes his or her last, that person's soul leaves its body and it passes from this world into the next. In the Bible, the word for 'spirit' is the same as the word for 'soul' and is also the same as the word for 'breath.'

"Remember, the Bible says that when Jesus died on the Cross, *Jesus cried out in a loud voice, "Father, into your hands I commend my spirit"; and when he had said this he breathed his last.'* (Luke 23:46) Afterwards, they took His body and placed it in a tomb, a burial place.

"The same thing happens when we die, we who are made in His image. When we breathe our last, our souls go on to the Father. The soul separates from the body and is taken to be judged by God. The body remains on earth and, for us Christians anyway, it's usually taken to a funeral home and prepared for burial."

"What's a soul? Is it in my breath?" asked a curious Ella, as she puffed air onto the palm of her hand.

"Oh, no. It's not your breath. A soul is what God gave each and every one of us to make us who we are and to make us like Him. The Bible teaches that God made man in His image and likeness. The soul is particularly unique for each person and links each person directly to God.

"Your soul is as much you as your body is you. While your body lets you do things like walk, talk, see, digest food, etc., your soul lets you think, love, make decisions, and, most importantly, lets you get to know God. Your body and soul were created by God and they belong to God for all eternity."

"Does it hurt to die?" asked Ted.

"I don't think so," said Grandpa Vernon. "For instance, Christina was in a lot of pain during her illness. Her entire body probably hurt. But when she died, or just before she died, all that sickness and pain left her body and her soul was set free. She became free of all earthly worries."

"Where is Christina now?" asked Ella.

"Christina's soul has passed on to the hands of the Father, to be judged worthy of entering heaven," replied Grandpa Vernon.

"Christina's body, on the other hand, has been taken to the funeral home. The funeral director will prepare her body for viewing and for burial. We will get to see her Thursday evening at what's called a 'visitation'—sometimes it's called a 'vigil' or a 'wake.' Understand that it's only her body we will be seeing. She will look peaceful, like she is sleeping in a big box lined with pillows. The box is called a casket or a coffin. But she won't be sleeping; there will be no waking her up. The visitation gives us a chance to see her one last time and to tell her family how much we loved her.

"On Friday, there will be a Funeral Mass at the church. After Mass everyone will go in a procession to the cemetery where Christina will be buried. Father Joseph will say the Mass and lead the prayers at the cemetery. All this time we should be praying that God is bringing her soul to heaven. But remember, even though her body is being buried there in the ground, her soul will already be on its way to Jesus."

"Do you think she is in heaven?" asked Danny.

"Oh, I suspect that she is," said Grandpa. "But only God knows for sure."

All three children looked at their grandpa with searching eyes.

"First and foremost, children, you must remember that Jesus died on the Cross for our sins and for our salvation," Grandpa Vernon began to explain. "He died so that our sins may be forgiven, thereby freeing us to enter heaven, our eternal reward.

"Clearly, when Jesus gave up His body in sacrifice on the Cross, He made us a promise that our sins may be forgiven, and as a result we could spend all eternity in heaven. But He really did leave the choice for getting to heaven up to each person.

"Let me read to you the words from the Gospel of Saint John," said Grandpa Vernon, reaching for his Bible. "We are told that not only is the promise of heaven ours because of Jesus' sacrifice, but that we have choices to make. We can live our lives in a manner in which we are worthy of heaven or we can turn away from God. Listen to this:

"For God so loved the world that he gave his only Son, so that everyone who believes in him might not perish but might have eternal life. For God did not send his Son into the world to condemn the world, but that the world might be saved through him. Whoever believes in him will not be condemned, but whoever does not believe has already been condemned, because he has not believed in the name of the only Son of God. And this is the verdict, that the light came into the world, but people preferred darkness to light, because their works were evil. For everyone who does wicked things hates the light and does not come toward the light, so that his works might not be exposed. But whoever lives the truth comes to the light, so that his works may be clearly seen as done in God." (John 3:16–21)

"The Bible makes it clear that Jesus, the light, made it possible for everyone to go to heaven, or as Saint John records, have eternal life. Unfortunately, not everyone's soul will go to heaven because some people, like Lucifer who was the fallen angel, prefer the darkness and evil works," said Grandpa.

"But how does it work?" begged Ella.

Grandpa explained, "When a person dies, his or her soul will be judged to determine if the person's love of God, their faith and actions on earth, are worthy of heaven.

"If a person dies and he or she has a pure soul, is free of all sin and imperfections, and is in a state of grace, then that person will be judged worthy of heaven and will be a saint from the very beginning of his or her new life. We believe they will go straight to heaven.

"However, the souls of those who have turned away from God and do not believe—which includes people who didn't follow the commandments, who freely choose evil over good, and who decided that they didn't want to know Jesus—like that devil Lucifer, these folks have condemned themselves. They will spend all eternity separated from God—or in other words, in hell or Hades or eternal fire—there are lots of words in the Bible that describe where they will be going.

"There are some people who will be judged worthy of heaven, but at the time of their deaths, their souls won't be quite perfect. It could be that they have venial sins that haven't been taken away, or they may hold on to some attractions to sinful ways, or for whatever reason, they aren't perfect enough to enter heaven. These folks' souls are destined for heaven, but they need to go through a purification process before entering. The place where the purification takes place, where all their imperfections are burned away, is called purgatory. Just how long it will take them to become perfect and enter heaven depends on their disposition at the time of death, and, very importantly, our prayers for them. That's why we pray for the poor souls in purgatory and have Masses said for those who have passed away. Prayers and Masses for the dead are very important."

"What if someone has sinned and done a lot of awful things in his or her life, but still somehow deep down loves Jesus and wants to be with God? Is there any hope for them?" questioned Ted.

"We always have hope that people like that find a way to turn to God, even if it is on their deathbed, and that God will forgive them," said Grandpa Vernon. "We can find a good example of this in the story of the good thief, Dismas, who was crucified with Jesus. Dismas sought God's mercy on the Cross, saying *'And indeed, we have been condemned justly, for the sentence we received corresponds to our crimes, but this man has done nothing criminal.'* Then Dismas said, *'Jesus, remember me when you come into your kingdom.'* And what did Jesus do? He showed him mercy. Jesus said, *'Amen, I say to you, today you will be with me in Paradise.'"* (Luke 23: 40–44)

"Does all this mean that only perfect souls are in heaven?" asked Ted.

"Yes," responded Grandpa Vernon. "There are only angels and saints in heaven."

"You mean that when Christina gets to heaven she will be a saint?" gasped Ella.

"That's true," said Grandpa Vernon. "She will be a saint, and she will be among the communion of saints when she gets to heaven."

"How long does it take?" asked an eager Ella.

"That I cannot answer. I do not even know if time after death is measured as we measure time on earth—in minutes, hours, days, weeks, and months. Only God knows the answer to that question. But I do know that our prayers help shorten the time, if any, that a soul has to spend in purgatory before becoming a saint."

A light seemed to go off in Ted's head. "Grandpa, isn't there another judgment at the end of the world, when our bodies get reunited with our souls?" he asked.

"Good question. I see you have been studying your catechism," said Grandpa Vernon. "At the very end of the world, when God decides it's the end, there will be a final judgment; sometimes it's called a general judgment. We acknowledge it every time we say the *Apostles' Creed:* 'He will come again in glory to judge the living and the dead. We believe in the Holy Spirit, the holy catholic Church, the communion of saints, the forgiveness of sins, the resurrection of the body, and the life everlasting.'

"At the end of the world, all bodies will be resurrected and reunited with their souls. People who have been judged worthy of heaven will have 'glorified' bodies—that means that their bodies will be free of illness and disease and won't be broken or blind anymore—they'll be perfect and beautiful, they'll be 'glorified,' and ready to experience the glory of God forever and ever. Those poor souls destined to hell—well, I expect their bodies will be putrefied, stinky, and rotten and no one, not even themselves, will want to touch them.

"At the last judgment, God will reveal to each and every one of us the good that we have done and failed to do and why we have earned entry into heaven or hell. From then on, I believe living in heaven will be like living in Paradise, or like the mansions your grandma used to dream about. Heaven will mean peace for all eternity. On the other hand—living in hell? Can you imagine living without God and without rules or truth or justice? Hell would mean pure misery for all eternity.

"Danny, hand me the Bible and let's look up what it says about how we will be judged when our time comes, and about purgatory," said Grandpa. For the next hour Danny, Ted, and Grandpa took turns looking up Scripture references and reading them out loud. Ella, who was too young to know how to read, was content to sit in Grandpa's lap and listen as he and her brothers took turns reading from the Bible.

Remembering Christina

"Can someone please help me with this tie?" pleaded Danny. It was Friday morning and the family was scrambling to get dressed and get to the church in time for Christina's Funeral Mass. Danny's fingers could not make the necktie go into a knot like he wanted. Besides, he was tired and he felt weird—kind of like a lump of worms was squirming in his stomach.

Danny prayed that the Mass and cemetery service today would go a lot better than the visitation last night. While he waited for someone to help with his necktie, Danny sat back and forced himself to remember the events of the previous night.

When they had arrived at the funeral home on Thursday it was nearly filled with people, more people than Danny expected to see. Some he recognized from church, some from town, but others were strangers—maybe out-of-town relatives of Christina's family. Mostly people were dressed in dark clothes, men in suits and ladies in dresses or suits, kids in their best clothes. He was glad he and his family had dressed up. A sign near the entrance let everyone know that Christina and her family were in the "Main Parlor," the biggest room in the entire funeral home.

The light in the Main Parlor was soft, like early dawn when the entire world is clearly visible but the sun hasn't made everything bright yet. Flowers and plants were everywhere and a sweet smell filled the room. At the far end of the room he could see a big polished wooden box surrounded by flowers and candles. He supposed that was the casket and that Christina's body was inside.

Everyone in his family but little Ella signed their names in a book, the Guest Book, and each one of them picked out a memorial card. The card had Christina's name on it, the dates of her birth and death, with her favorite prayer printed on one side and a picture of Jesus on the other. Danny thought it would make a good bookmark if he kept it nice and didn't mess it up, so he put the memorial card in the pocket of his sports jacket for safekeeping.

Lots of people were standing in line to greet Christina's parents and her two sisters. When Danny's family approached Christina's mom, she went to Danny's mom and gave her a big hug. Both mothers started crying. Danny couldn't remember the last time he saw his mother cry. All of a sudden, he felt like he should be crying, too. Then Christina's mom hugged him, and Ella and Ted, too. Before Danny could say anything she took them by their hands and walked them up to the casket where Christina lay. Danny wasn't sure he was ready for this, but he peeked inside the casket and saw Christina, looking beautiful and very peaceful. For sure all her pain and sickness were now gone.

Danny and Ted knelt beside the casket to say a prayer. Grandpa Vernon had told them that was what you were supposed to do. However, Ella jumped up on the kneeler, reached in, and gave Christina a poke. Then she touched Christina's hand and called her name: "Christina! Hey, Christina!"

"Grandpa, you were right—Christina's body is dead. She doesn't move and she's cold!" blurted Ella in a loud whisper that almost everyone in the funeral home could hear. "I bet her soul is already in heaven. Don't you think so, Grandpa?"

Danny was so embarrassed that he wanted to turn and run. How could a sister of his do and say such a thing at a time like this? Didn't she remember her manners? What should he do—what words should he use to apologize? He looked up in fear at Christina's mom, only to find that she had a smile on her face and a chuckle in her throat.

"It's okay, Danny. If the tables were turned, Christina would have done and said something just like that, or maybe even worse! Kids, huh?" said Christina's mother. "It's good that Ella and you boys understand about death. Did your Grandpa tell you all about dying and how souls get to heaven?"

"Yes, he did. I am sorry about your loss and I offer my condolences," said Danny, struggling with the word "condolences". "Grandpa explained things to us and told us what to say and how to act. I am really sorry about Ella—I guess she wasn't paying attention to the part on 'how to behave'." With that Danny grabbed Ella and pulled her away from the casket before she could do or say anything more embarrassing.

"I would like you children to go into the next room and join the other children who came tonight," said Christina's mother. "We'd like you to do something special for us. Ms. Kelly, the religious education teacher from church, is in the room and she is helping the children create a memorial of Christina's life. We want the memorial to be ready to put out before the Funeral Mass tomorrow. You children knew Christina better than almost anybody else, so you would be a big help in creating the memorial. Will you do that for me?"

Danny was relieved to have a reason to leave the room and to take big-mouthed Ella with him.

Ms. Kelly had the children organized in teams according to their ages—preschoolers, kindergartners, and first graders in one group, and the older children in another group.

She suggested that the little kids draw pictures of the things they liked to do with Christina, or remember the last time they were with Christina and draw a picture of what they did on that day. "Perhaps you played in the yard, went swimming, climbed a tree, played with dolls. . ."

"We always played dolls together," interrupted Ella. "I can draw that picture."

"Wonderful," said Ms. Kelly. "Here are the pencils, colored markers, pens, and paper. I even have some colored paper, scissors, and glue in case you want to create a picture rather than draw one. When you are finished, please sign your name at the bottom of your picture. I will help you if you don't know how to write your name. Then we will put all the pictures on a big bulletin board and give it to Christina's parents, okay?"

The younger children were thrilled with their assignments and got right to work. Danny was happy that Ella had something to do that kept her quiet and out of the Main Parlor of the funeral home.

"Christina's parents have asked the rest of you boys and girls to write a letter and tell them of a favorite memory you have of Christina or describe what you liked to do together," instructed Ms. Kelly. "If it is easier to tell it in pictures, please feel free to draw a picture or create a collage. You might describe a time you were together at a picnic, went for a walk in the woods, listened to music, or just sat on her front porch swing. Maybe you were a friend of one of her sisters, but that doesn't mean you don't have a favorite memory—something nice or funny or even sad that you did with Christina."

Danny looked over Ella's shoulder while she was working on her picture. It looked like she was drawing herself playing with Christina, pushing their doll buggies. The picture showed two stick figures walking down a sidewalk in front of some houses. The sun was a big yellow ball above their heads and brightly colored blobs indicated flowers beside the walkway. She even drew a bubble-headed boy who looked like he was about to jump out at them from behind a tree. Danny was sure the bubblehead was him because he was almost always pestering the girls. The last thing Ella did was to draw a big house sitting on top of a cloud in the sky.

"What's that?" asked Danny.

"That's the mansion that God gave her to live in—in heaven," replied Ella. "You know, like the one He gave Grandma!"

"That's really nice, Ella. Really special." A little while earlier he had wanted to disown his sister, but now Danny hugged her with brotherly affection and pride.

Now it was Danny's turn to prepare a memorial to Christina. He wrote a letter from his heart:

To Christina's Mom and Dad,

Christina was my good friend and neighbor. Christina was kind and generous and liked to memorize her prayers. She knew more prayers than me, even though she wasn't in my grade. I liked to tease her and she liked to tease me back. She had a pure heart and I know she must be with God.

Love,
Danny

Ted's memorial to Christina, a picture and just a few words, described her entry into heaven. He drew a little girl walking into a gigantic arena, like a huge football stadium. Oh, how Ted loved sports! In his picture, the stadium was filled with angels and saints, cherubim and seraphim, and music notes floated in the air over the stadium.

The top of Ted's picture read:

TODAY CHRISTINA PASSED ON TO
JOIN GOD'S ROOKIE SAINT TEAM
Love,
Ted

Ms. Kelly had prepared three large bulletin boards. She pinned the picture drawn by Ella in the middle of the little kids' board. Then she pinned the other little kids' drawings around Ella's. She did the same with Danny's and Ted's contributions to the memorial. When the bulletin boards were finished, the older boys carried them out to the Main Parlor and placed them on easels placed beside Christina's casket.

Christina's parents cried a lot when they saw all the pictures and read the letters. But they smiled and laughed a lot too. The memorials seemed to make both her mom and dad feel better, and they were very appreciative.

After most people had had a chance to look at the memorials, Father Joseph knelt beside Christina's casket and led them in saying the Rosary. Danny had learned to say the Rosary when he was getting ready for his First Communion. He even kept a rosary in the pocket of his good sport coat, just like his dad always did. He was prepared. He felt a lot older this night.

When they got home from the funeral home, Danny's mom fixed soup and salad and toasted cheesy bread for the family to eat. He felt kind of hungry, but not in the usual way—his stomach was confused. His mom told him that he should eat anyway, that it would make him feel better. He did eat, and he did feel better. How had she known that?

During the night, Danny felt lonely and got up to crawl into bed with his parents. Before morning, both Ella and Ted did the same thing, and got into their parents' big bed too. It just felt like the right thing to do, to be close together as a family.

Grandpa Stumbles

The next morning, Grandpa Vernon interrupted Danny's thoughts with an offer he could not refuse. "Come here, young man, and let me teach you how to tie a necktie!"

"Thanks, Grandpa. I just never remember which way the long end goes," said Danny as he adjusted his thoughts to prepare for the day ahead of him.

Christina's Funeral Mass was a new experience for Danny, Ella, and Ted. It wasn't like a normal day in church. Flowers filled the front of the church where Christina's casket was covered with a white cloth, called a pall, and placed by the altar. It seemed like everyone in the entire town had turned out for her Funeral Mass.

In his homily, Father Joseph tried to explain that today was a day of both great sadness and great joy. He said that above all, today was a day of celebration of a life that was beautiful and complete. He explained that for Christina's friends and family, her life might have seemed way too short. But in God's eyes, Christina's life on earth was just the right length of time.

Danny understood what Father Joseph said to be the truth, even though it was hard to accept. Other people must have had a hard time accepting it, too, because many of them were crying—but not Ella, Christina's best friend. Ella kept asking why people were crying, but he figured she was too young to really understand.

Six boys from the upper grades were chosen to be the pallbearers, the people responsible for placing the casket in the hearse, and later carrying it into the church and then to the gravesite at the cemetery. Christina's casket wasn't very large or heavy, so it was easy for the boys to carry it.

The school's music teacher, Sister Mary Rose, was in charge of the music performed at Christina's Funeral Mass. It was a lot like the beautiful sacred music played and sung for Sunday Mass, but today, the middle school's chorus made up the choir. Ted was a member of the chorus, as he had a really nice singing voice. During Communion time, he sang the *Ave Maria* all by himself. Danny was very proud of his brother and thought he was really brave to sing in front of all those people.

After Mass, everyone headed toward the cemetery. The shiny black hearse led a procession of cars that followed in a line that seemed to reach all the way across town. The staff of the funeral home placed small flags on all of the mourners' cars to let other drivers know that this was a funeral procession and that they should stop driving to let the cars pass. The coolest part was that there were police stationed at all the major intersections on the route to the cemetery, blocking traffic to allow the funeral cars to drive right through red lights. Christina would have loved seeing this, thought Danny.

When they got to the cemetery, the pallbearers carried the casket to the gravesite and placed it on a rack over a deep hole already dug in the earth. Everyone gathered around, and then Father Joseph said more prayers and sprinkled the casket with holy water.

As Father Joseph was talking, Danny looked around the cemetery and felt a peacefulness that he hadn't felt in days. The sun shining through the green trees made a lacy shade over Christina's gravesite. The birds were chirping, and a pair of squirrels chased each other around a tree. "If your body has to be somewhere waiting to be reunited with its soul, this place isn't a bad choice," thought Danny.

"Christina's family invites you all to join them for a luncheon in the parish hall at the conclusion of this commitment rite," announced Father Joseph.

"And now, may almighty God bless you, the Father, the Son, and the Holy Spirit. Go in peace to love and serve the Lord. This concludes our service."

People started to walk toward their cars. They were walking away from Christina, leaving her all alone in the little casket! Danny felt a panic come over him, then suddenly felt a hand on his shoulder. He looked around—and saw Grandpa Vernon walking just behind him.

"Aren't they going to put her body in the ground?" asked Danny, with a troubled look on his face.

"The staff from the funeral home and the cemetery will tend to that, after we leave. They'll be careful and respectful as they tuck her into the ground—don't worry," said Grandpa Vernon.

"That's a creepy job," said Danny.

"Oh, not really," said Grandpa. "It takes a special love and devotion to do a job like that—God bless them. Why don't we come back and visit Christina's grave after the luncheon? Your grandma's grave is just on the other side of the cemetery. Maybe you'd like to go with me to visit and say a prayer for her today, too."

"I'd like that very much," said Danny.

As they began walking toward the car, Grandpa seemed more slouched over than usual—and then suddenly, he stumbled.

"Are you okay, Grandpa?" asked Danny, grabbing his arm to steady him.

"Oh, yes. I'm just feeling a little more tired today than usual," said Grandpa. "I'm sure I'll feel better after lunch."

Time Passes

The days and weeks following Christina's funeral passed by pretty much as normal. Danny was amazed that the world went on and people seemed to go about their business as usual. It was almost as if it didn't matter that Christina was gone. That just didn't seem right to him. Often when he thought about her, he wanted to shout—"She was here!" Then he would feel sad. His parents as well as Father Joseph said it was normal to feel confused and sad when someone close to you dies. It was part of something they called "grief." Everybody said that over time he would feel less confused and less sad—but he wasn't so sure about that.

"Danny, sometimes I really miss Christina," confessed Ella. She was sitting with her brother on the front steps waiting for their mom to bring Grandpa Vernon back from his doctor's appointment. "But sometimes I even have a hard time remembering what she looked like or what she sounded like. Why is that?"

"I don't know why, Ella. But I know what you mean. Sometimes I try to remember her, but it's hard," said Danny. "I'm really glad we made that memorial for her at the funeral home. Her mom kept all of those pictures and letters, you know. I bet she would let you look at them whenever you want. She'd probably like you to come over for a visit."

"Yeah, I bet she would," said Ella. "I am going to ask for permission to go over there as soon as Momma and Grandpa get home."

Just then, the station wagon pulled into the driveway. Danny and Ella ran up to greet their mother and grandfather. Danny watched as Grandpa struggled to get out of the passenger side—his shoulders were slumped and his eyes looked tired. "What's the matter with him?" Danny thought to himself.

"Hi, Grandpa! How was the doctor? What did he do to you? Did he stick you with a needle?" Danny peppered him with questions.

"Oh hi, kids. It's good to be home. The doctor just ran some tests and things. Yes, he stuck me with a needle to do some blood work. You know how I hate that! Then he joked with me about getting old. And then we talked some more," said Grandpa Vernon. "And now, if you don't mind, I'd like to go to my room and rest. I'll tell you more after dinner."

Danny's stomach felt as if it was filled with those squirming worms again as he watched Grandpa Vernon walk slowly into the house. As much as he didn't want Grandpa to come live with them in the first place, now he couldn't bear the thought of him not being there—Grandpa was definitely a part of the family. In fact, Grandpa Vernon had become his best friend.

After dinner, Grandpa Vernon seemed his old self again—full of energy and stories. When the table was cleared and the dishes done, he and the kids retreated to the attic for another evening of adventure stories.

Grandpa Vernon began to tell them the story about the time he and their grandma stopped a thief on the island of Saint Thomas in the U.S. Virgin Islands.

"We were living on board our boat, First Lady, while anchored at the harbor by the city of Charlotte Amalie and waiting for the hurricane season to end," he began. "Who can find the Virgin Islands on that old globe?"

The Virgin Islands are off the coast of Florida, in the Caribbean Sea, which looks to be part of the Atlantic Ocean. As usual, Ted was the first to spot a location on Grandpa's globe, quickly finding the Virgin Islands and pinpointing the harbor where his grandparents must have anchored.

"Every morning your grandma would head for shore in the dinghy—that's a small rowboat. We kept the dinghy tied to the big boat and used it to go ashore to shop for dinner or go to church or to do whatever we needed to do on the island," explained Grandpa Vernon. "When you live on a boat on the water, you need a way to get to shore—only Jesus and Peter could walk on water, you know!

"Most days, I'd get up after Grandma had already taken off for town in the dinghy. I'd usually see an empty cup and dish on the stern (that's the back end of the boat), and figure she'd just left her empty cup and toast plate there for me to clean up. It wasn't her habit to leave dirty dishes sitting around, but I didn't think much of it. Anyway, on those days I'd clean her dishes and then make myself breakfast. Then I'd spend my time fixing things on the boat. Boats always need to have something fixed. Well, one day, Grandma asked if I liked the breakfasts she had been leaving for me. She seemed disappointed that I never said "thank you" or complimented her on the nice breakfast. Well, that's when we realized that someone must have been stealing my breakfast. There was a thief in Charlotte Amalie harbor!

"The next morning I got up early with her, but I stayed inside the cabin. I watched her put out my breakfast and then leave for shore in the dinghy. I set myself up to keep watch—I had a good view of the stern from where I stood in the galley inside the boat, but no one could see me. After she had been gone about ten minutes, I heard a little splash in the water near the stern.

When I peeked out the galley way, I saw a small dark hand reach up and take the piece of toast.

"Slowly, very slowly, I crept out of the galley way, into the cockpit, and looked over the transom. Aha! I grabbed the thief's wrist just as his hand was reaching for some fruit.

"When I looked down, I saw that I was holding onto the arm of a young native child, a little boy no older than seven or eight. Oh, he struggled to get away, but I was strong then, and I was able to haul the kid onto the deck with just one hand. Once I got him onboard, I saw that he had on swimming trunks and was outfitted with snorkel and mask on his face and swim fins on his feet. He obviously had been swimming under water so as not to make noise and then slithered up on the transom at the back of the boat where he could sit unnoticed until it was safe to reach up and snatch the breakfast. A clever little thief!

"Turns out that both his parents went to work early in the morning, leaving him to fend for himself. One day, as he was swimming around the harbor, he saw my breakfast and, being hungry and not knowing much about right or wrong, couldn't resist. After that he would swim around in the harbor nearly every day, and when my breakfast appeared he'd just help himself!

"Well, I gave a lecture to the boy about stealing, but it seemed to go in one ear and out the other. However, in time I got him to understand that it is wrong to take something that belongs to another person. Once he understood, he said he was really sorry for what he did.

"After we got right versus wrong straightened out, your grandma started leaving two breakfasts in the morning, one for me and one for him. The boy, Moses was his name, would come by, and he and I would eat our breakfasts together, then I would teach him some things—and he taught me stuff too. He was very smart and learned fast. He helped me fix the boat, and asked me questions about the world beyond the Virgin Islands. Some days we would talk about God, and I taught him his prayers. His parents were happy to have someone looking after the boy. They were Catholic, but didn't go to church very often."

"What happened to Moses?" asked Ted.

"He turned out pretty well, as a matter of fact," said Grandpa Vernon.

"We've kept in touch over the years. At the time your grandma and I were leaving Saint Thomas, Moses had just enrolled in the private Catholic grammar school on the island. He excelled in school. With the help of some generous people and scholarships, he was able to go to Florida to attend high school and college. Moses became a doctor and now he has a very successful medical practice on the island of Saint Thomas. He also started a recreation center to keep local children out of trouble. He calls it his 'payback' for being saved from a life of crime."

"Grandpa, you are a hero!" exclaimed Ella.

"Thanks, Ella. But, I'm not a hero. I always aim to do the right thing because that's what God asks us to do."

Grandpa Vernon picked up the Bible and handed it to Danny. "Danny, please read to us from Micah 6:8. It's one of my favorite passages."

Danny opened the Bible to the Old Testament Book of Micah and began to read. "It says, *'You have been told, O man, what is good, / and what the LORD requires of you: / Only to do the right and to love goodness, / and to walk humbly with your God.'*"

"That's the lesson for tonight—always do what is right, love goodness, and walk humbly with God. Now, you kids need to say your prayers and get to bed," said Grandpa Vernon. "And me, too!" Grandpa Vernon sighed as a veil of tiredness seemed suddenly to cover his face.

"Grandpa Vernon, you haven't told us about the doctor," said Danny, reminding him of his promise from earlier in the day.

"Well, Danny, I don't want to scare you," began Grandpa Vernon.

Danny immediately felt tears stinging and welling up in his eyes. Just hearing the words "I don't want to scare you" scared Danny a lot.

"In truth," continued Grandpa, "the doctor says that my disease has not improved with the treatments he's given me. There isn't another treatment that he can give to someone my age. However, it is a slow-moving disease, so

I'm not in danger of dying anytime soon. But death is not something I fear because I live in the joyful hope of seeing Jesus face to face. I hope you all can appreciate that."

Danny tried hard not to cry over what he had just heard, but then a big sob overcame him. Grandpa Vernon gathered him in his arms and kissed his head. "It will be okay. Do not worry and do not be afraid. Besides, I am still here and I have a lot more stories in me, got that?" he assured the boy.

"You aren't afraid to die?" asked Ella, placing her arms around her grandpa's neck.

"No, I'm not," he responded. After thinking about it for a second he said, "Often we are afraid when we face something new. For instance, I was afraid when I set off to sail around the world, and when I first thought about scuba diving, and before I asked your grandmother to marry me—now that was really scary.

"But each time I prayed for God's help, and put my trust in Him to keep me safe and guide me along the way—and He did. Now I pray that Jesus will guide me through this new voyage to reach His kingdom, to get to heaven. It's all rather exciting, actually, and I am ready when He is."

Anointing of the Sick

"Hurry, or we'll be late for church! Children, this is a special Sunday, as Grandpa is going to receive the Anointing of the Sick this morning," urged Mrs. Walsh.

All three children were struggling to share the mirror and sink in what had become the "children's bathroom." Danny was trying to tie his necktie while Ted was combing his hair. Ella was pretending to wash her hands, but mostly she just liked getting in her brothers' way.

They left the bathroom one by one and gathered together in the living room to wait for their mother and grandfather to finish getting ready for church. "What's Anointing the Sick?" asked the ever curious Ella.

"Anointing of the Sick is a sacrament that is given to people when they are sick but it is also given to people who are growing old and may have gradually failing health," explained Mr. Walsh.

"Grandpa is sick, you know. His illness is pretty much under control, but he is slowing down. Fortunately he's not in any danger of dying soon, not that we know of, anyway—that's for God alone to know. But because of the disease and his age, the priest has suggested that Grandpa receive the special sacrament for the sick. Father Joseph will administer the sacrament during Mass today. There will be other people receiving the sacrament along with your grandpa."

"Will it make him feel better?" questioned Danny.

"Perhaps. The Sacrament of the Anointing of the Sick will give your grandfather special graces and gifts of the Holy Spirit to guard against anxiety, discouragement, and temptation and to give him peace and fortitude," explained their father. "Sometimes just having your soul more at peace helps a person's body to feel better and to recover. Let's offer our Mass today for Grandpa Vernon's health and spiritual well-being."

Danny had seen with his own eyes that over time Grandpa Vernon's health was getting worse, and that he was weaker. A couple of months ago, Danny's parents moved Grandpa's room downstairs so he wouldn't have to climb the stairs every day. Grandpa's room was now what was once the den, and the den was moved upstairs to what was Danny's old room. Grandpa Vernon didn't go with them to the attic as often anymore either, only when he had enough energy. And those days were getting fewer and farther in-between.

Sunday Mass started pretty much the same way it always did. But then Father Joseph began to offer special prayers for the sick. After the homily, Father recited a litany of prayers for those who were sick, and for the people who cared for them. Danny felt included as he and the whole family cared for Grandpa Vernon.

Father Joseph invited those who were to receive the Anointing of the Sick to come to the front of the church along with their families and friends. Some of the people who came forward, like Grandpa, looked old and tired. Some were in wheelchairs, and some had to sit down because they were too weak to stand. To Danny's surprise, there was even a pregnant lady and a young girl there to receive the Anointing of the Sick. Later, Danny's mom explained that the pregnant lady was having complications in her pregnancy and that is why she needed the Anointing of the Sick. The little girl was going into the hospital on Tuesday for a serious operation. "We're all different, but we all need God's help," Danny's mom had said.

Danny watched intently as Father Joseph said a prayer over the jar of oil that had been removed from a cabinet near the altar called an ambry. Danny had learned while preparing for his First Communion that oils consecrated by the Bishop on Holy Thursday were kept in the ambry.

Father Joseph next approached each person who was there to receive the sacrament, placed his hands on his or her head and prayed quietly. Recalling Jesus' own usual manner of healing, the priest recited from the Gospel of Luke, Chapter 4: *"At sunset, all who had people sick with various diseases brought them to him. He laid his hands on each of them and cured them."*

Then the priest took some of the oil from the jar and made the Sign of the Cross on each one's forehead, saying: *"Through this holy anointing may the Lord in his love and mercy help you with the grace of the Holy Spirit."*

Everyone in the church responded: "Amen."

Next, the priest used the oil to make the *Sign of the Cross* on the palms of the sick people's hands and said: *"May the Lord who frees you from sin save you and raise you up."*

Again, all responded: *"Amen."*

After that, Father Joseph had the people go back to their seats and he continued saying Mass in the usual way.

That was pretty simple, thought Danny. He looked at Grandpa Vernon—he didn't look any different on the outside, but he knew he was different on the inside—inside his soul. Through the action of the Holy Spirit he had been given new grace. Danny started thinking that all the sacraments are really pretty simple, but they impart a powerful amount of grace. He was glad he was here today.

Danny's parents had invited Father Joseph to have dinner with them this Sunday after Mass. While Mrs. Walsh was preparing to put dinner on the table, she asked Danny, Ted, and Ella to show Father Joseph around the house, which they did with great enthusiasm. They liked having company in the house, and Father Joseph was "special" company.

Father seemed particularly impressed with Danny's aquarium, and the way the boys had decorated their room in a nautical theme. The children could not resist taking Father Joseph up to their attic getaway, and telling him about the evenings they used to spend there with their grandfather.

"Do you want to talk about what happened in church today and about what your grandfather is experiencing?" asked Father Joseph. He made himself at home in the attic, sitting in Grandpa Vernon's stuffed chair, and the children pulled up their chairs around him.

Danny was the first to ask a question. "You said this morning during Mass, that Anointing of the Sick was a sacrament of healing. But mom and dad tell us that there is no cure for Grandpa's disease. How can he be healed?"

Father Joseph replied, "Danny, there are different types of healing. The most important is the healing of the soul, which is what this sacrament is meant to do. The Anointing of the Sick heals by imparting grace to overcome the difficulties that go along with being sick, difficulties like despair, self-pity, giving in to the temptations of sin. It also provides for the forgiveness of sin if the person receiving the sacrament, because of his or her illness, hasn't been able to go to confession. We have to be willing to accept the grace in order for it to work. Sometimes physical healing happens along with the spiritual healing."

"Who made up the sacrament?" Ella asked next.

"This sacrament, as all our sacraments, was instituted by Jesus Christ," answered Father Joseph. "The Bible describes the miracles performed by Jesus and, not surprisingly, most of the miracles involved healing. The healing that Christ performed was sometimes physical in nature, but it always involved healing of the soul and deepening of the faith. There are many examples in the Bible. There's the story of Christ healing Peter's mother-in-law (Matthew 8:14–15), the lady who was healed by just touching the tassel of Jesus' cloak (Matthew 9:20–22), the cripple at the pool outside the Temple (John 5:5–15), and many others. In Luke's Gospel (Luke 5:18–19), we learn that one time a group of people was so anxious to have Jesus cure their paralyzed friend that they cut a hole in the roof of the house where Jesus was staying and lowered the sick man down to Him!

"Jesus even gave his Apostles the authority to heal. *He summoned the Twelve and gave them power and authority over all demons and to cure diseases, and he sent them to proclaim the kingdom of God and to heal [the sick].'* (Luke 9:1–2) That is very important, as it paved the way for allowing me to carry out the sacrament that I did today."

"Will Grandpa Vernon go to heaven?" Ted asked, probably already knowing the answer but still wanting to hear Father Joseph's opinion.

"I pray that he does," smiled Father Joseph. "You tell me why you think he will go to heaven," he said, turning the question back over to the children.

"Because he was good and he taught us all about God," blurted Ella.

"Yes. What else?" asked Father Joseph, looking at Ted.

"Because he prayed a lot, believed in God, and always did the right thing," answered Ted.

"Yes. Those are important reasons. But there is one very important reason. Here's a clue! Without this there would be no heaven for your Grandpa Vernon or anyone else."

"I know!" shouted Danny. "Because Jesus died on the Cross for him and for all of us. Jesus died so our sins could be forgiven and so that we might live forever with Him."

"That's it!" exclaimed Father Joseph, pleased with the response.

Then Father Joseph explained that the sacrament of Anointing of the Sick nearly eliminates the prospect of going to hell. This seemed to the children like really good news, but before they could explore other mysteries of faith, Mrs. Walsh called them for dinner.

Food for the Journey

It was late fall. It was crisp and cold outside, and the trees, earth and sky had all turned gray. There was even a flake or two of snow in the air. Danny thought he could feel the grayness as he walked home from school. When he rounded the corner in front of his house, he noticed a different car in the driveway. Nobody told him that his parents were expecting company. He was puzzled.

When he opened the front door, Danny saw his mother standing at the doorway to Grandpa Vernon's room. Next to her stood Father Joseph. Danny's heart began beating hard and fast. Was Grandpa near death? Danny knew that the plan was to call Father Joseph when Grandpa's illness got worse.

"But not today, not now!" a voice inside Danny's head screamed.

Seeing the panic on her son's face, Danny's mom reached out to him and said, "I'm glad you're home. I called Father Joseph and asked him to come this afternoon because I think Grandpa Vernon is failing. He has been dozing on and off since morning, and he doesn't want anything to eat or drink. I think he may soon be passing on."

Danny was glad to see his grandfather awake and lying in bed, but his worry showed on his face. His mother hugged him and Father Joseph put his hand on his shoulder to comfort him. The priest put a purple stole around his neck, like the one he wears when he hears confessions.

"Why don't I go sit with Vernon while you wait for the others to arrive home," suggested Father Joseph. "That way, if he wakes up and wants me to hear his confession, I will be by his side. When the entire family is here, I will give Vernon the Anointing of the Sick again, then Holy Communion. This will probably be his Holy Viaticum."

While Father Joseph sat with Grandpa Vernon, Danny and his mother went into the kitchen to wait for the rest of the family. Danny desperately hoped the others would be home soon.

"What's Viaticum?" asked Danny.

"Viaticum comes from the Latin and means 'that which you take on the road'—it's the provisions for the journey," explained Danny's mother. "It is the last Eucharist a person receives before he or she passes on. It will prepare your grandfather to pass over from this world to the Father. You probably remember from your First Communion class, learning the words of Jesus,

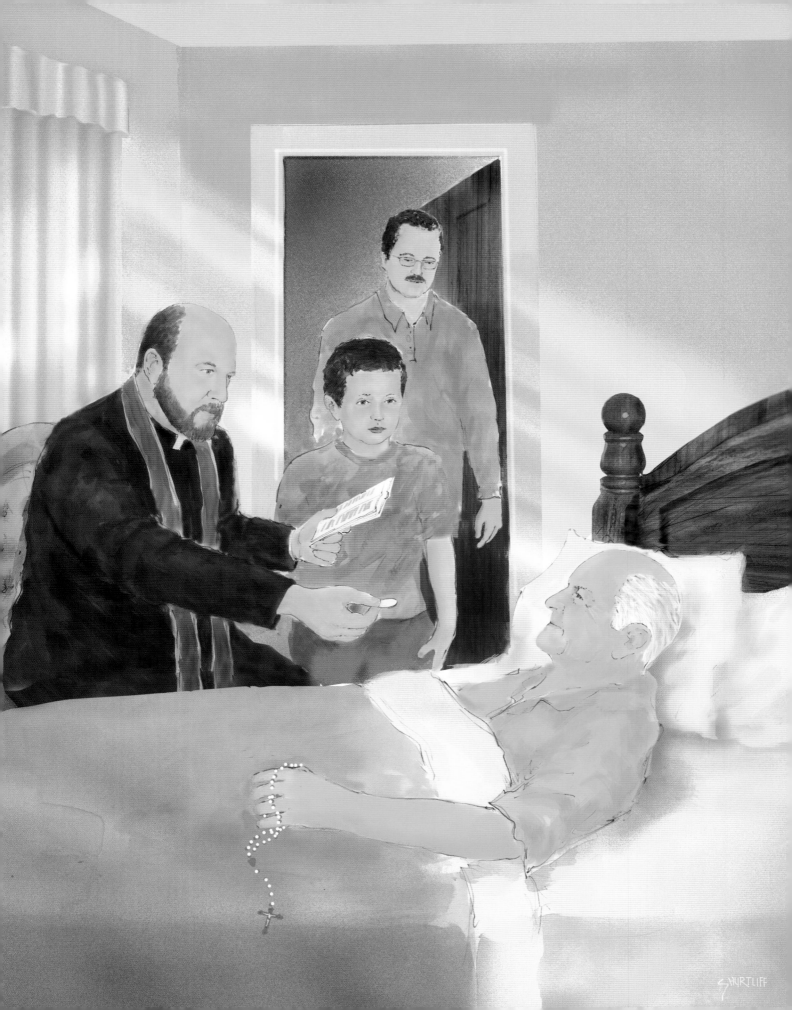

'Whoever eats my flesh and drinks my blood has eternal life, and I will raise him on the last day.' (John 6:54) The Holy Viaticum, the last Holy Communion, is the Body, Blood, Soul, and Divinity of Jesus, and it will carry your beloved Grandpa Vernon on his journey from this place on earth to our Father in heaven.

"You know how much your grandpa loved the Lord. The Holy Viaticum is a beautiful way for him to prepare to meet God and to join in the Communion of Saints."

"I guess if it helps him to be with God, then it has to be all right," said Danny. "But I don't want him to die. I will miss him a lot."

"None of us want that. But if God calls Grandpa, it's God's will," said his mother. "We will all miss him. But right now, we should be happy and thank God that we can be with Grandpa as he begins his most exciting journey—his last voyage."

"Mom, I am so glad that you made me give up my room so Grandpa could live with us. Thank you." Danny gave his mother a big hug.

Within the hour, the family all gathered by Grandpa Vernon's bedside. He was awake and alert, and understood that Father Joseph was there to give him his last rites. Father began by sprinkling them all with holy water, and then made the *Sign of the Cross,* saying, *"In the Name of the Father, and of the Son, and of the Holy Spirit."*

In an odd way, the sprinkling of holy water reminded Danny of Baptism.

Next Father Joseph read some Scripture and led them in prayers. They even prayed for all the other sick people in the parish. "That's a pretty nice thing to do," thought Danny.

Danny watched as Father preceded with the Anointing of the Sick. Just like he did in church months earlier, Father Joseph anointed Grandpa Vernon's head and the palms of his hands with oil. He said some more prayers, and then they all said the *Our Father* together. Danny silently prayed that the anointing would strengthen Grandpa's body as well as his spirit.

Danny was happy to see that Grandpa was able to sit up to receive Holy Communion. He felt sure that the anointing had given Grandpa strength.

Father Joseph finished with a blessing, they all made the *Sign of the Cross,* and the service was ended. Danny didn't want it to end because he liked having Father Joseph around and because he was afraid of what might happen next.

"There is nothing more I can do here," said Father Joseph. "Take turns sitting with Vernon tonight. You might want to talk to him about the things you did together, about the special times in your lives, and tell him how much you love him and appreciated him sharing his life with you here in this house. Pray with him and for him."

"We'll read the Bible to him, he likes that," offered Ella.

"That's a great idea, Ella," said Father Joseph. "I will keep you all in my prayers. Call me if you need anything more," he said as he walked out the door.

All evening long, the family kept a vigil at Grandpa Vernon's bedside. Sometimes they would all be in his room at the same time, and sometimes just one of them would be there. They would talk to each other, talk to Grandpa, and sometimes just sit quietly.

Danny felt a real calmness come over the house. There wasn't the usual hustle and bustle, just peacefulness. From time to time he heard his mom and dad talk about "arrangements" and when they should call out-of-town relatives. But Danny felt surprisingly at ease with his feelings for the first time in a long time.

A little before midnight, only Danny and Ted were in Grandpa's room when he sat up and looked at them, smiled, and then stared out into the doorway. "Look boys, there she is. There's your grandmother. Isn't she beautiful! And there's little Christina standing beside her. Wave to her, boys, wave to Christina. I'm coming, ladies."

Danny and Ted looked toward the empty doorway, then they looked at each other in total confusion. "Oh-Oh! You better go get mom and dad," Ted whispered to Danny.

With that, Grandpa Vernon laid back down on his pillow. He had a smile on his face and a look of complete happiness.

All of the family was now together in the room, and heard Grandpa Vernon take a couple of deep breaths and exhale slowly. Then he took another deep breath. It seemed he held it for a long while, but then Danny noticed he quietly exhaled. Danny knew immediately that Grandpa Vernon had passed away, and that his soul was on its way to the Father, to eternal rest.

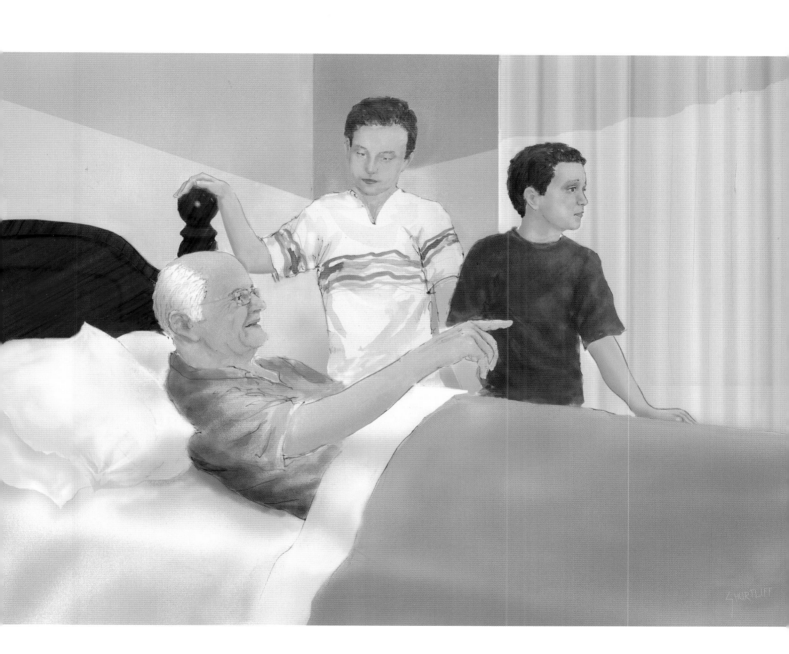

Remembering Grandpa Vernon

"This house is just crazy. I thought we were supposed to be quiet after someone died. I feel like I'm in the middle of a zoo and all the animals are out of their cages," said Danny in frustration.

It was morning and there were a lot of people in the house. Friends, neighbors, and even people who were complete strangers to Danny kept calling and coming by with food—casseroles and bread and hams and baked chickens, even cookies and cakes.

It was so peaceful the night before when Grandpa Vernon passed away. Danny wanted it quiet again so he could think. He liked that it was just their family present when his grandfather died—he didn't want to share that part of his life with anyone else.

After Grandpa passed away, two men from the funeral home came and took his body away. They all cried because it was really sad, but nothing else could be done. To comfort everyone, Danny's mom made buttered toast and hot chocolate. It was almost three o'clock in the morning before Danny got to bed. He could not remember ever staying up that late. The phone started ringing around nine a.m. the next morning, and then people started arriving at the house. Now Danny felt grumpy and out of sorts.

"Children, this is Moses Reynolds, an old friend of your grandpa's. He is going to be staying here with us. He wants to help out," said Danny's mother.

"Moses!?" exclaimed Danny. Ted and Ella were nearby and stopped in their tracks when they heard the name Moses. Before them stood a tall, handsome, dark-skinned man. This was the legendary Moses from Charlotte Amalie Harbor on the island of Saint Thomas.

"Do you know him?" asked their mother. She was surprised because she knew that they had never met Moses before now.

"Grandpa told us about him," said Danny. "They were friends from Grandpa and Grandma's sailing days."

"He was a thief!" exclaimed Ella. "He stole Grandpa's breakfast. But Grandpa taught him right from wrong and then he became a doctor."

Moses chuckled over Ella's introduction. "Yes, your grandfather was a very good influence on me. I came all the way from the Virgin Islands to show my respects to him. I am pleased to meet members of his family."

As they talked with him some more, Danny thought Moses was terrific, a really great man. Moses even reminded Danny of Grandpa, especially when he talked about the times they shared in Charlotte Amalie. He must have learned to tell stories from Grandpa, because he was really good at it.

Later Moses made lunch for them from the food the neighbors brought. Afterwards he assured the children, "I am here if you need anything—anything at all. In the meantime, I would like to be useful by making phone calls to let other friends know about your grandfather's passing."

Danny, Ted, and Ella retreated to the attic to escape all of the people and craziness in the kitchen and living room. "Will we get to make a memorial for Grandpa Vernon at the funeral home, like we did for Christina?" asked Ella. "I want to make something to remember him."

"No, they don't do things like that for grownups, only kids," said Ted.

"So, why don't we create our own memorial?" suggested Danny. "It's not like we have anything else to do. Besides, it'll be fun. Dad said we won't be going back to school until after Grandpa is buried."

"Great idea," said Ted. "We'll need some paper, pencils, scissors, paste, colored markers, and tape. I know where there is a big bulletin board that we can use for displaying our memorial. Hopefully we can put it up in the church during visitation. Let's bring the stuff up here to the attic to work on it—no one will know we are making it and it'll be a surprise!"

From time to time, the children would take a break from their work. Danny would spin the old globe, put his finger on it to stop it spinning, and then retell Grandpa Vernon's stories about that particular place. His brother and sister encouraged him to write down some of the stories and make them part of the memorial.

Ted liked to thumb through Grandpa's old Bible, and would find cards, pressed flowers, and little notes stuck there, between the pages. Grandpa Vernon had told stories about why he kept those things in the Bible. These little mementos were important to Grandpa, and Ted decided he should write down their stories, too.

When Ella got bored, she pulled things out of the old trunks that held Grandpa Vernon's things and she told her brothers what Grandpa had said about each thing. It was almost as if she was telling the whole story of her grandparents' lives. The boys decided they should help Ella to write down her memories.

When the memorial was finished, the children stood back to admire their work—then Ted noticed something was missing.

"I have to add the last story," said Ted. "It won't be ready until tomorrow before the service." Then he disappeared into the upstairs den to work on the missing piece.

The morning of Grandpa Vernon's funeral finally came, and the house was quiet for a change. Danny felt the same heaviness in his stomach that he had on the day when Christina was buried. As he put on his suit, he wished Grandpa was there to help with tying his tie.

The visitation took place in the church before the Funeral Mass and the casket had been placed at the end of the nave. It was flanked by candles and flowers. A beautiful flower arrangement was on top of the casket, on the lower half. The upper part was open so you could see Grandpa Vernon lying inside. Grandpa didn't look like himself, but that was okay. Danny had pictures and lots of memories that were much better than seeing him lying there in the casket.

The children's parents were impressed with the job they had done on their grandfather's memorial, and were very proud. Just before the people started to arrive, Danny and Ella helped Ted bring in the bulletin board memorial they had made and set it at the head of the casket. Then Ted pulled a piece of paper from a folder and pinned it to the center of the board. It was a picture similar to the one he drew for Christina's memorial. But in this picture, Grandpa Vernon was standing in front of the gates of the giant stadium filled with angels and saints. In the stands, waving to Grandpa and welcoming him to heaven, Ted had drawn figures of Grandma and little Christina! Jesus was there in the picture, too! Ted had titled the picture:

TODAY SOMEBODY WE LOVE PASSED AWAY!
BE WITH GOD, GRANDPA VERNON

Love,
Ted, Danny, and Ella

Epilogue

Many years have gone by. It is Ella's wedding day, and she is beautiful as she walks down the aisle. She is wearing the same veil and bridal gown that her grandmother wore on her wedding day nearly sixty years earlier. Danny and Ted serve as witnesses, as Ella and her new husband exchange vows in celebration of the Sacrament of Holy Matrimony.

Danny, now a grown man, moves his hand up to straighten his tie. A spark of electricity runs through his body as he suddenly remembers when he was just a little kid and how Grandpa Vernon taught him to tie his tie.

Ted, too, has a flood of memories when he sees their sister so beautiful in that old wedding dress. The boys, now men, think of their beloved grandfather. Danny recalls their visits to the attic and the great adventure stories that Grandpa Vernon shared with them. He still has a picture in his mind of little Ella trying on that veil and posing in front of Grandpa Vernon's mirror. What wonderful times! Then with deep gratitude, Danny remembers how his Grandpa made the acceptance of death and eternal salvation so meaningful for his grandchildren.

A smile crosses Danny's face as he considers the meaning of the vows that his sister and her husband are now reciting . . . *"until death do we part."*

He prays that Ella and her husband will have as long and as fulfilling a marriage as their grandparents before them.

THE END

Some Final Things

Prayers of Comfort

SIGN OF THE CROSS

In the name of the Father, and of the Son, and of the Holy Spirit. Amen.

❧

OUR FATHER

Our Father, who art in heaven, hallowed be Thy name; Thy kingdom come; Thy will be done on earth as it is in heaven. Give us this day our daily bread; and forgive us our trespasses, as we forgive those who trespass against us; and lead us not into temptation, but deliver us from evil. Amen.

❧

HAIL MARY

Hail Mary, full of grace! The Lord is with thee; blessed art thou among women, and blessed is the fruit of thy womb, Jesus.

Holy Mary, Mother of God, pray for us sinners, now and at the hour of our death. Amen.

❧

GLORY TO THE FATHER

Glory be to the Father, and to the Son, and to the Holy Spirit. As it was in the beginning, is now, and ever shall be, world without end. Amen.

❧

ACT OF CONTRITION (VERSION 1)

O my God, I am heartily sorry for having offended Thee, and I detest all my sins, because I dread the loss of heaven and the pains of hell, but most of all because they offend Thee, my God, who art all good and deserving of all my love. I firmly resolve, with the help of Thy grace, to confess my sins, to do penance and to amend my life. Amen.

❧

ACT OF CONTRITION (VERSION 2)

O My God, I am sorry for my sins with all my heart.
In choosing to do wrong and failing to do good, I have sinned against You whom I should love above all things. I firmly intend, with Your help, to do penance, to sin no more, and to avoid whatever leads me to sin. Amen.

❧

THE APOSTLES' CREED

I believe in God, the Father Almighty, Creator of Heaven and earth;
and in Jesus Christ, His only Son, our Lord,

who was conceived by the Holy Spirit, born of the Virgin Mary,
suffered under Pontius Pilate, was crucified, died and was buried.
He descended into hell; on the third day He rose again from the dead.
He ascended into heaven, and sits at the right hand of God, the Father Almighty;
from thence he shall come to judge the living and the dead.
I believe in the Holy Spirit, the Holy Catholic Church,
the communion of saints, the forgiveness of sins,
the resurrection of the body, and life everlasting. Amen.

PRAYER FOR THE SICK

Dear Jesus, Divine Physician and Healer of the sick, we turn to You in this time of illness. O dearest comforter of the troubled, alleviate our worry and sorrow with Your gentle love, and grant us the grace and strength to accept this burden. Dear God, we place our worries in Your hands. We place our sick under Your care and humbly ask that You restore Your servant to health again. Above all, grant us the grace to acknowledge Your will and know that whatever You do, You do for the love of us. Amen.

LITANY OF COMPASSION FOR THE SICK

We pray with special love and concern for all those who are ill or infirm, asking the Lord for His consoling grace to strengthen the sick in times of trial.
Response (R.): Lord, be close to give your comfort
When pain or distress is overwhelming, R.
When the healing process goes slower than hoped, R.
When terrified by treatments or therapy, R.
When it's hard to let go of long-held plans, R.
When the feeling of alienation arises, R.
When worn out and weary, R.
When troubled by impatience and negativity, R.
When loneliness adds to anxiety, R.
When sickness makes it difficult to communicate, R.
When discouragement or despondency sets in, R.
When fear makes it impossible to face the future, R.
When the ravages of disease attack self-esteem, R.
When anger and resentment assail, R.
When beset by worry or fretfulness, R.
When it's hard to rely on others for care, R.
When envy arises towards those who are healthy, R.
When pessimism or cynicism holds sway, R.
When anguish is intensified by the need for reconciliation, R.
When sickness is mistaken for punishment, R.
When loved ones are far away, R.
When sickness causes financial hardship that leads to worry or despair, R.

When afflicted by the feeling of nothing to hope for, R.
When weakness makes it impossible even to think, R.
When friends draw back fearful of disease, R.
When illness makes those who are suffering moody or irritable, R.
When haunted by regret and the shame of past sins, R.
When it's difficult to sleep, R.
When there's loss of appetite, R.
When there's resistance to necessary change, R.
When tempted by denial, R.
When nobody seems to understand, R.
When bound to home or when restricted in movement, R.
When listlessness and apathy threaten, R.
When medication seems to make things worse, R.
When all that's needed is a caring touch, R.
When it's impossible to maintain familiar routines, R.
When it's hard to find the strength to go on, R.
When it becomes difficult to pray, R.
When suffering of any sort becomes hard to bear, R.
When death draws near, R.
Our Father . . .
Most merciful Father, your beloved Son showed special compassion to lepers, tenderness to those long sick, and healing to the infirm laid before Him. We place before You all those who are ill and in need of healing grace. May the love and mercy of the Divine Physician raise up all who suffer from sickness and restore them to health and peace. We ask this in the name of Jesus. Amen.

A Short Prayer for the Dying

O, Saint Joseph, foster father of the Child Jesus and true spouse of the Blessed Virgin Mary, pray for us and for the dying of this day (or this night). Amen.

Prayer For the Dying

Almighty and merciful God, You bestow on mankind both the remedies of health and the gifts of everlasting life. Look graciously on your servant suffering from bodily infirmity, and strengthen the soul which You have made. At the hour of his death may he deserve to be offered without stain of sin to You his Creator by the hands of the holy angels. Through Christ our Lord. Amen.

At the Last Hour

Blessed Joseph, who yielded your last breath in the loving embrace of Jesus and Mary, when the seal of death shall close my life, come, Holy Father, with Jesus and Mary to aid me, and obtain for me the one solace I ask for that hour, to die encircled by their holy arms. Into your sacred hands, living and dying, Jesus, Mary, and Joseph, I commend my soul. Amen.

❧

Prayer to St. Joseph for a Happy Death

O, blessed Joseph, who didst die in the arms of Jesus and Mary, obtain for me, I beseech thee, the grace of a happy death. Defend me from the attacks of my infernal enemy in that hour of dread and anguish, to which I now invite thee, that thou mayest assist me by thy presence and protect me by thy power. Obtain of our dear Lord that I may breathe out my soul in praise, saying in spirit, if I cannot utter the words: Jesus, Mary, and Joseph, I give you my heart and my soul. Amen.

❧

Prayer for a Happy Death (Venerable Bede)

If it so pleases my Maker, it is time for me to return to Him who created me and formed me out of nothing when I did not exist. I have lived a long time, and the righteous Judge has taken good care of me during my whole life. The time has come for my departure, and I long to die and be with Christ. My soul yearns to see Christ, my King, in all His glory. Glory be to the Father, and to the Son, and to the Holy Spirit. Amen.

❧

For One Recently Deceased

Incline Your ear, O Lord, to our prayers, in which we humbly entreat Your mercy. Bring to a place of peace and light the soul of Your servant, (N.), which You have summoned to go forth from this world, and bid him to be numbered in the fellowship of Your saints. Through Christ our Lord. Amen.

❧

Prayer for the Faithful Departed

O gentlest Heart of Jesus, ever present in the Blessed Sacrament, ever consumed with burning love for the poor captive souls in Purgatory, have mercy on the soul of Thy servant, (N.). Be not severe in Thy judgment, but let some drops of Thy precious Blood fall upon our beloved departed, and do Thou, O merciful Savior, send Thy angels to conduct the soul of Thy servant to a place of refreshment and peace. Amen.

❧

Responsorial for All the Faithful Departed

V. Eternal rest grant unto them, O Lord.
R. And let perpetual light shine upon them.
V. May their souls and the souls of all the faithful departed, through the mercy of God, rest in peace.
R. Amen.

Scripture References

On the Sacrament of Anointing of the Sick

A sacrament is an outward sign established by Jesus Christ to confer inward grace. The sacrament of the Anointing of the Sick conveys God's grace to the recipient through the power of the Holy Spirit, to bring spiritual and even physical strength during an illness. An ordained priest or bishop administers the sacrament. The New Testament provides for the promulgation and authority of administering the sacrament.

Jesus sent out these twelve after instructing them thus:, "Do not go into pagan territory or enter a Samaritan town. Go rather to the lost sheep of the house of Israel. As you go, make this proclamation: 'The kingdom of heaven is at hand.' Cure the sick, raise the dead, cleanse lepers, drive out demons. Without cost you have received; without cost you are to give." (Matthew 10:5–8)

He summoned the Twelve and began to send them out two by two and gave them authority over unclean spirits. . . . So they went off and preached repentance. (Mark 6:7, 12)

They drove out many demons, and they anointed with oil many who were sick and cured them. (Mark 6:13)

He summoned the Twelve and gave them power and authority over all demons and to cure diseases, and he sent them to proclaim the kingdom of God and to heal [the sick]. (Luke 9:1)

However, some Jews from Antioch and Iconium arrived and won over the crowds. They stoned Paul and dragged him out of the city, supposing that he was dead. But when the disciples gathered around him, he got up and entered the city. On the following day he left with Barnabas for Derbe. (Acts 14:19–20)

Is anyone among you sick? He should summon the presbyters of the church, and they should pray over him and anoint [him] with oil in the name of the Lord, and the prayer of faith will save the sick person, and the Lord will raise him up. If he has committed any sins, he will be forgiven. (James 5:14–15)

On God's Judgment

When a person dies, his or her soul passes from the body, goes before God, and receives a particular or individual judgment. Through this judgment, the person will know his or her eternal destiny—heaven or hell.

A second judgment, a general or last judgment, occurs at the end of time when Jesus returns. At the general judgment, all souls will be reunited with their resurrected bodies and God will reveal to each and every one of us why we have earned entry into heaven or hell for all eternity. The Bible gives us insight on how these particular and general judgments might happen and how the consequences of our earthly actions will destine us to eternal joy or eternal damnation.

"Just so, every good tree bears good fruit, and a rotten tree bears bad fruit. A good tree cannot bear bad fruit, nor can a rotten tree bear good fruit. Every tree that does not bear good fruit will be cut down and thrown into the fire. So by their fruits you will know them.

"Not everyone who says to me, 'Lord, Lord,' will enter the kingdom of heaven, but only the one who does the will of my Father in heaven. Many will say to me on that day, 'Lord, Lord, did we not prophesy in your name? Did we not drive out demons in your name? Did we not do mighty deeds in your name?' Then I will declare to them solemnly, 'I never knew you. Depart from me, you evildoers.'" (Matthew 7:17–23)

"I tell you, on the day of judgment people will render an account for every careless word they speak. By your words you will be acquitted, and by your words you will be condemned." (Matthew 12:36–37)

"The Son of Man will send his angels, and they will collect out of his kingdom all who cause others to sin and all evildoers. They will throw them into the fiery furnace, where there will be wailing and grinding of teeth. Then the righteous will shine like the sun in the kingdom of their Father. Whoever has ears ought to hear." (Matthew 13:41–43)

"Again, the kingdom of heaven is like a net thrown into the sea, which collects fish of every kind. When it is full they haul it ashore and sit down to put what is good into buckets. What is bad they throw away. Thus it will be at the end of the age. The angels will go out and separate the wicked from the righteous and throw them into the fiery furnace, where there will be wailing and grinding of teeth." (Matthew 13:47–50)

"Then he will say to those on his left, 'Depart from me, you accursed, into the eternal fire prepared for the devil and his angels." (Matthew 25:41)

"And these will go off to eternal punishment, but the righteous to eternal life." (Matthew 25:46)

Do not be amazed at this, because the hour is coming in which all who are in the tombs will hear his voice and will come out, those who have done good deeds to the resurrection of life, but those who have done wicked deeds to the resurrection of condemnation. (John 5:28–29)

On Purgatory

Nothing unclean will enter the presence of God in heaven! (Revelation 21:27) How, then, does a person who dies still holding on to some imperfections enter into heaven? His or her soul must go through a purification process so as to achieve the holiness necessary to enter the joy of heaven. The Church gives the name purgatory to this final purification of the elect who will enter heaven. The need for final purification and the reasons for prayers for the dead are rooted in the Old and New Testaments.

They all therefore praised the ways of the LORD, the just judge who brings to light the things that are hidden. Turning to supplication, they prayed that the sinful deed might be fully blotted out. The noble Judas warned the soldiers to keep themselves free from sin, for they had seen with their own eyes what had happened because of the sin of those who had fallen. He then took up a collection among all his soldiers, amounting to two thousand silver drachmas, which he sent to Jerusalem to provide for an expiatory sacrifice. In doing this he acted in a very excellent and noble way, inasmuch as he had the resurrection of the dead in view; for if he were not expecting the fallen to rise again, it would have been useless and foolish to pray for them in death. But if he did this with a view to the splendid reward that awaits those who had gone to rest in godliness, it was a holy and pious thought. Thus he made atonement for the dead that they might be freed from this sin. (2 Maccabees 12:41–46)

"Therefore, if you bring your gift to the altar, and there recall that your brother has anything against you, leave your gift there at the altar, go first and be reconciled with your brother, and then come and offer your gift. Settle with your opponent quickly while on the way to court with him. Otherwise your opponent will hand you over to the judge, and the judge will hand you over to the guard, and you will be thrown into prison. Amen, I say to you, you will not be released until you have paid the last penny." (Matthew 5:23–26)

"If you are to go with your opponent before a magistrate, make an effort to settle the matter on the way; otherwise your opponent will turn you over to the judge, and the judge hand you over to the constable, and the constable throw you into prison. I say to you, you will not be released until you have paid the last penny." (Luke 12:58–59)

[For] no one can lay a foundation other than the one that is there, namely, Jesus Christ. If anyone builds on this foundation with gold, silver, precious stones, wood, hay, or straw, the work of each will come to light, for the Day will disclose it. It will be revealed with fire, and the fire [itself] will test the quality of each one's work. If the work stands that someone built upon the foundation, that person will receive a wage. But if someone's work is burned up, that one will suffer loss; the person will be saved, but only as through fire. (1 Corinthians 3:11–15)

[For] we all fall short in many respects. If anyone does not fall short in speech, he is a perfect man, able to bridle his whole body also. (James 3:2)

May the Lord grant mercy to the family of Onesiphorus because he often gave me new heart and was not ashamed of my chains. But when he came to Rome, he promptly searched for me and found me. May the Lord grant him to find mercy from the Lord on that day. And you know very well the services he rendered in Ephesus. (2 Timothy 1:16–18)

Strive for peace with everyone, and for that holiness without which no one will see the Lord. (Hebrews 12:14)

For Christ also suffered for sins once, the righteous for the sake of the unrighteous, that he might lead you to God. Put to death in the flesh, he was brought to life in the spirit. In it he also went to preach to the spirits in prison, who had once been disobedient while God patiently waited in the days of Noah during the building of the ark, in which a few persons, eight in all, were saved through water. (1 Peter 3:18–20)

If anyone sees his brother sinning, if the sin is not deadly, he should pray to God and he will give him life. This is only for those whose sin is not deadly. There is such a thing as deadly sin, about which I do not say that you should pray. All wrongdoing is sin, but there is sin that is not deadly. (1 John 5:16–17)

[But] nothing unclean will enter it, nor [anyone] who does abominable things or tells lies. Only those will enter whose names are written in the Lamb's book of life. (Revelation 21:27)

Funeral Customs and Traditions

The story about the passing of Christina and Grandpa Vernon that opens this book describes and explains customs and traditions embraced by the Catholic Church. Other world religions may follow similar traditions and customs, or observe very different ones. It is important to know how others deal with the passing of loved ones, so that you can be of comfort to those of different faiths. The following information should help you know what to expect and to show the proper respect when someone of another faith passes. To help to understand the difference between Catholic customs, traditions, and beliefs and those of other religions, some comparisons and contrasts are included.

Non-Catholic Christians/Protestants

Funeral traditions of non-Catholic Christians, i.e., Protestants, vary from one denomination to another. Some of the more traditional sects (e.g., Anglican, Episcopalian, Lutheran, Methodist, Presbyterian) have much in common with Catholicism with regard to funeral rites. The similarities include the means of notification (obituary), arrangements coordinated through a funeral home, times set aside for visitation, funeral services held in churches, and interment/inurnment in a cemetery. Sometimes Protestant families favor holding the funeral service or memorial service in a funeral home, its chapel, a private chapel, or a public meeting place, rather than in a particular church.

The order of a Protestant funeral is similar to a Catholic funeral. If the body has not been cremated, a visitation or wake is usually held the night before the funeral, where prayers are said and memories may be shared. The visitation is also a nice way to allow those who are unable to attend the funeral (often held during the day when many adults are working) to say goodbye. The funeral service itself begins with a hymn or other religious music. The minister greets the congregation and begins the ceremony with a prayer. Either a minister or an attendant reads passages from the Bible. The minister may lead the congregation in more prayers, offer a reflection on death or on the person's life, and allow some silent time for personal reflection. Other hymns may be sung, a eulogy given, or memories shared. The service in the church ends with the minister commending the deceased to the mercy of God. The mourners are invited to proceed to the gravesite where the person's body is committed to the earth.

All Christians, Catholic and non-Catholic, believe in Divine judgment, heaven, hell, justification, salvation, and the resurrection and glorification of the body. These are fundamental Christian beliefs and they give form to the grieving process and the rituals of the funeral.

Some Protestant sects believe that the departed are assured of salvation through faith alone, whereas Catholics believe that, as sinners, they are never fully assured of salvation, but confidently and joyfully hope for it. As Saint Paul said, "Work out your salvation in fear and trembling" (Philippians 2:12). All Christians believe that the soul passes from the hands of loved ones on earth to the hand of God, through Jesus Christ. Catholics, however, express great sympathy for the deceased who, on passing, are judged according to their works (Romans 2:6). Catholics hold that the Funeral Mass and other prayers for the dead, in which God's mercy is called upon to bring the deceased through death into life eternal in His presence (1 John 5:15-17), lessen the time that the deceased would otherwise have to endure in purification through purgatory.

This difference may explain why Protestant funeral services sometimes take on more of a celebratory nature. Loved ones are sad that the deceased is no longer with them, but they are also happy for the deceased, since they believe that he or she is with God.

Judaism

When a Jewish person is close to death, his loved ones surround and comfort him. He confesses his sins in preparation for death. A vigil or watch immediately follows the moment of death. A person, called a shomer, is assigned to keep watch over the body and recite psalms until burial. This duty may be given to more than one person.

As preparation for burial, the body of the deceased is ritually cleaned and "purified" with water. The body is then dressed in white shrouds and, if the deceased is male, wrapped in his tallit, or prayer shawl. Shards of broken pottery are placed on the eyes and mouth, recalling the destruction of the Temple. Earth from Israel is sprinkled over the body, representing a Jew's link to the Promised Land and the ancient covenant. Caskets are not tightly sealed so that the body will return to dust, as God told Adam. (Genesis 3:19) Caskets are not open for viewing at any time during the funeral ceremonies. Burial is to take place within twenty-four hours of death.

In all burial ceremonies, respect for the body is very important, hence cremation is not permitted. Belief in the resurrection of the body is a debated issue in Judaism. Orthodox Jews and some Conservative Jews believe in it, but Reform Jews (the largest body of Jews in America) and Reconstructionist Jews reject this belief.

The actual funeral service is typically short and simple, consisting mainly of a psalm being read and eulogy being given. Pallbearers carry the casket to the gravesite, stopping symbolically seven times along the way. The casket is then lowered into the ground and mourners cover it with dirt, using the backside of a shovel. After this, the Mourners' Kaddish, a traditional blessing, is recited.

Mourning is an essential part of burial and certain mourning practices are obligatory for the immediate family members. Prior to the funeral, family members are to tear a visible piece of clothing to symbolize the rending of their hearts.

The first seven days after burial are referred to as shivah. These are days of intense mourning when the family members remain at home in quiet bereavement. Music is not played, men do not shave, mirrors are covered, wine is not drunk, among other practices. Friends and family members may come to the house during this time, offering their condolences and bringing food for meals. Visitors should not initiate any greeting or conversation, but should merely be there for the mourner. This custom of visiting is called sitting shivah.

The thirty-day period after the burial is called shloshim. These days after shivah are marked by similar acts of sorrow and a somber disposition. Mourners may return to work and should participate in synagogue (Jewish house of worship), but all celebratory events should be avoided.

The entire year following burial, called shana, is also a time of mourning, but life gradually returns to normal.

Islam

The funeral ceremony for a deceased Muslim (a person of the religion of Islam) is similar in many ways to a Jewish funeral ceremony. The burial is to take place within twenty-four hours of death, if possible. Prior to this, the body is to be ritually washed by close friends or family. The body is then wrapped in a white shroud and placed in a temporary casket with the head turned facing Mecca (the holiest city in Islam, located in Saudi Arabia). If a Muslim who has died is considered a martyr, however, he is not wrapped in a shroud, but buried in the clothes in which he or she died. Cremation is forbidden. Belief in resurrection of the dead is firmly held.

After the body is prepared for burial, it is carried to the mosque (the place of worship for Muslims) for prayers that are led by the imam, the figurehead of the mosque or "preacher." All participants must undergo ablution, or ritual cleansing. Prayers are then said and passages of the Koran are read aloud. After these prayers are said, there is a somber procession to the cemetery. At the gravesite, the body is lowered into the ground as more prayers are recited.

It is Islamic custom to bury the dead directly into the earth, without a casket. If local law requires a concrete coffin or vault, it will be filled with earth, and then the deceased is buried in the earth inside the container with the head elevated slightly by a stone or a brick and turned towards Mecca. Mourners then fill in the grave with dirt. Any decoration or extravagance of either the body or the gravesite is considered to be non-Islamic.

After burial, loved ones observe three days of mourning. These days are marked by increased devotion, receiving visitors into the home of the family, and a generally solemn mood. Widows are to observe a mourning period of four months and 10 days. During this time, the widow is not to remarry, move, or wear jewelry.

Hinduism

Hindus believe in reincarnation, or that the soul is placed into another body, either animal or human, after death. This migration of the soul is a path along the way to nirvana, an otherworldly spiritual happiness. According to Hinduism, the person who actively pursues this end through contemplation and by renunciation of bodily pleasures (actually a rejection of all earthly things) attains nirvana. On account of this belief, death in Hinduism is not considered a sad event. Hindus view death as part of an ongoing journey through life, and every death is the beginning of a new life.

Although Christians also believe that the end of this life brings on the beginning of another life (whether in heaven, hell, or, for a time, purgatory), for Hindus it is a completely different understanding. Hindus believe that you become a different person after death. For them, the love, knowledge, and memories that you have in one life do not follow you into the next life. For Christians, your love, knowledge, and memories become an essential part of who you are, and you retain these in eternal life.

The Hindu belief in reincarnation differs significantly from Christian beliefs. Hindus believe the deceased soul is placed into another body (either human or animal), whereas Christianity teaches that human nature (as opposed to the nature of, say, a dog or cat) is an essential part of who we are.

A Hindu funeral ends with a ritual burning of the body, rather than burial. Upon death, the body is cleaned and dressed in traditional white garments. The funeral then is a procession to the crematorium during which the line of mourners may pass places that were significant to the deceased. Once at the crematorium, the body is decorated, scriptures are read, kindling is lit, and prayers are said. For Hindus, the act of cremation releases the spirit from the body.

Prior to returning to the family's home, the mourners bathe and change their clothes. Afterwards, there is a meal and more prayers are said. This begins a thirteen-day period of mourning, during which friends and family visit and offer condolences.

Buddhism

Like Hindus, Buddhists also believe in reincarnation and nirvana. Consequently, for Buddhists, death is both the end of something and the beginning of something. The dying person's focus should be on having the right state of mind, which consists in overcoming all desire. Buddhism teaches that a person will continue to be reincarnated as long as he desires anything. The highest Buddhist virtue, then, consists in escaping the reality of this world. This is very contrary to Christianity, which teaches that everything that God created is good and our desire for these created things is also good, so long as we desire them in the proper way.

There are many and varied Buddhist funeral traditions, since Buddhism is more of a system of thought and belief than it is a formal religion. Buddhists believe that the body is merely a shell for the soul, and so generally there are no elaborate rituals at Buddhist funerals. This does not mean, however, that death is unimportant. Death is one of the most important Buddhist life cycles, since it exemplifies the Buddhist teaching that all of life is suffering. A Buddhist monk officiates at the funeral ceremony in which prayers are said, and readings are recited. The body is almost always cremated in imitation of the Buddha.

The great disparities of traditions among the Buddhist sects (e.g., Theravadin Buddhists to Mahayana Buddhists to Vajrayana Buddhists), however, make it impossible to generalize about the ceremony itself. The most important theme in all Buddhist funeral rites, though, is that death is part of an endless cycle. One dies and is reborn hundreds of times throughout his life, until he escapes from this cycle and attains nirvana.

Non-Religious

Because atheists, or secular humanists, do not believe in an afterlife, their funerals take on a very different mood. The focus is entirely on the life that the person has lived. It is meant to be a celebration and memorial of that person, though it often turns into a reflection on what the person's life meant to the attendants. From a Christian perspective, it is difficult to understand the grieving process of atheists. Their emotions cause them great sadness and they remember all of the special moments in the person's life, but at the same time, they generally assert that life is meaningless, the mere product of chance. Atheists will often say that the deceased person "lives on" in the minds and memories of those he or she touched.

The atheist, or humanist, "funeral" is a relatively new, or at least a newly popularized, phenomenon. In times past, an atheist may have commonly received a religious funeral at a church, perhaps the church he attended as a child or that family members attended. This created an awkward, uncomfortable, and often impossible situation for the loved ones and clergy, who knew that the deceased did not believe in God and was not a religious person.

Today, funerals for atheists/humanists feature their own rituals, associations, and officials. A humanist funeral may consist of some of the following: music, reflection on death, poetry readings, a eulogy, an opportunity to share memories of the person, candle lighting, moments of silence, etc. A funeral director, layperson, or public official leads the ceremony, using care not to say anything that might offend a believer or non-believer. The deceased person's body is either buried or cremated. A memorial service sometimes takes place at the burial site, a public meeting area, or the crematorium. There are no formal processes for grieving or offering condolences.

Glossary of Terms and Phrases

Fortunately, it's not often that someone we know dies or that we are expected to participate in a funeral service. When we don't do things very often, sometimes the practices and words used are unfamiliar and can be confusing. The following definitions should help you to prepare for and get through a funeral.

ANOINTING OF THE SICK—The Sacrament given to people who are gravely seriously ill, have serious health problems, are about to undergo surgery, are elderly, or whose health status is declining. (See the chapter titled Anointing of the Sick.)

ARRANGEMENTS—The coordination of all activities that must take place after someone dies. Often the funeral home director or mortician works closely with the family to be sure that all details are covered.

CASKET OR COFFIN—A special box used to hold the body of the deceased. It may be made of wood or metal and lined inside with soft padded material. Most caskets have handles on the sides so that the pallbearers can carry it in and out of the church and to the cemetery.

CEMETERY—The place of burial or entombment. Some cemeteries are owned and maintained by a church, some are public cemeteries run by cities, townships, or counties, and others are privately owned. Individuals purchase the right to be buried in a grave, entombed in a crypt, or, after cremation, have their ashes placed in a niche in a cemetery.

COMMITTAL SERVICE—The ceremony at the gravesite that concludes the funeral. It is an acknowledgement that the deceased's earthly journey is complete, but that the journey to eternal reward has begun. Friends and family of the deceased gather as prayers or final words are said around the casket. In some traditions, a family member will place the first shovelful of dirt onto the casket. In other traditions, family and friends may throw flowers into the grave.

CONDOLENCES—Expressions of sympathy offered to the immediate family, co-workers, and close friends of the deceased. Words of condolence may include phrases like: "I am sorry for your loss . . . my deepest sympathies . . . please accept my most sincere condolences on the loss of (name). . . you have my heartfelt sympathy, my prayers are with you and with (name)." If you do not know the person to whom you are offering condolences, it is appropriate to introduce yourself and tell how you were related/acquainted to the deceased, e.g. "Hello, my name is Danny. I was a friend of Christina's from school. Please accept my condolences." Keep it short. Let them ask you questions if they feel like it.

CONSECRATED GROUND—Catholics are to be buried or entombed in consecrated ground or crypts. Consecrated means a Bishop has blessed the cemetery in a special ceremony. Many public and private cemeteries have sections that have been consecrated where Catholics may be buried.

CREMATION—The body is reduced to ashes in a special place called a crematorium. The ashes are placed in a box or urn for final interment.

CRYPT—An above-ground burial chamber. The casket is placed inside the crypt and the crypt is closed and sealed.

EMBALMING—The process the funeral home uses to prepare a body for burial.

EULOGY—A speech given at a funeral by a family member or close friend of the deceased that recalls specific aspects of the deceased's life. At a Catholic Mass, the eulogy is given at the conclusion of the Mass, before the final blessing. Eulogies are not to be given after, or in place of, the homily.

FUNERAL—A series of events that take place leading up to, and on the day of interment. Traditions and customs vary by religions and ethnic cultures (see the section on Funeral Traditions). The funeral may include any or all of the following: visitation (vigil or wake) at the funeral home, viewing, closing of the casket (usually reserved for immediate family), procession from funeral home to church or synagogue or mosque, service at the church (which includes the Mass of Christian Burial for Catholics), service at the funeral home or chapel (for non-Catholics with no particular church affiliation, and for non-believers), procession to the cemetery, committal service, closing of the grave, and lunch after the funeral.

FUNERAL HOME—The place where the body of the deceased is taken to prepare it for visitation, the funeral, and burial. The funeral home staff usually is available to assist the family in many other ways, including selecting a casket, coordinating with the cemetery, placing obituaries in the newspaper, ordering flowers, scheduling the services, providing cars, arranging for memorial cards, creating online memorials, etc.

GRAVE—The hole in the ground where the deceased is buried. The typical grave is three feet wide and eight feet long and up to six feet deep. The grave is "opened" (dug) by people working at the cemetery before the funeral. A vault is placed inside the grave by the funeral home staff and then the casket holding the deceased is placed inside the vault. The vault is sealed and the earth is replaced over the vault.

GRAVESTONE (ALSO CALLED MEMORIAL MARKER OR HEADSTONE)—The monument or plaque, usually made of stone, which is engraved with the deceased's name and dates of birth and death, and is usually placed on top of and at the head of the grave, crypt, or niche.

GRIEF—The feelings people experience when a person or animal/pet they love has passed away. The feelings usually include shock, denial, anger, sadness, and, over time, acceptance.

HAPPY DEATH—Dying in a state of grace and in communion with Jesus Christ and the saints.

HEARSE—The vehicle used to transport the body of the deceased to and from the funeral home, church, and cemetery.

IMMEDIATE FAMILY—Usually includes parents, brothers, sisters, spouses, and relatives that live in the same house as the deceased.

INTERMENT—The placing of remains into their final resting place, such as a grave, tomb, crypt, or niche.

LUNCH AFTER THE FUNERAL—The deceased person's immediate family usually invites mourners to gather for lunch after a funeral or memorial. This allows the family and friends to visit and reminisce about the deceased and have some nourishment after a stressful ordeal.

MAUSOLEUM—A burial chamber that contains one or more crypts for interment above ground. Some mausoleums are quite large and have rows and rows of crypts stacked four or five high.

MEMORIAL CARD—Cards that are offered to mourners during the funeral home visitation or at the funeral. The birth date and date of death are usually printed on the cards along with a prayer, poem, or saying.

MEMORIAL SERVICE—Similar to a funeral service, except that the body of the deceased is not present.

MORTICIAN OR UNDERTAKER—A person who works for the funeral home and who helps get the deceased's body prepared for the visitation and funeral. Morticians are specially trained and licensed to perform their work.

MOURNER—Any person attending a funeral home for visitation or attending a funeral service for a deceased.

NICHE—An alcove into which an urn containing the cremated remains of the deceased may be placed. It is similar to a small crypt.

OBITUARY—A notice placed in the newspaper or on the internet about the person who died. The notice often identifies members of the immediate family and includes information about the deceased (birthplace, education, work, hobbies, military service, etc.), the location and hours of services, where to send flowers or donations instead of flowers. A picture of the deceased may be included with the obituary.

OPEN CASKET—A phrase used to indicate that the lid of the coffin (usually just the upper half) is open during a visitation so the mourners can see the face of the deceased one last time. Being able to view the body often helps mourners to accept the reality of death.

PALL—The white cloth that is put over the casket during the Funeral Mass. The white pall is a symbol of Baptism and belief in the Resurrection.

PALLBEARER—A person chosen to help carry the casket during the funeral. In processions, the pallbearers ride behind the hearse so they are ready to assist in carrying the casket when the hearse reaches the funeral home, church, or cemetery. Typically there are six or eight pallbearers, usually men or older boys. It is an honor to be asked to be a pallbearer.

URN—A container used to hold the ashes of a deceased person who was cremated.

VIATICUM—It is the last Eucharist a person receives before death. For more information, read the chapter Food for the Journey in this book.

VAULT—A burial chamber that is placed in a grave and into which the casket is placed. Vaults are usually required by law because bodies cannot be buried directly in the earth. For those religions whose tradition requires the deceased be buried in earth, the vault is filled with earth (instead of a casket) and the deceased is buried in the earth inside the vault.

VISITATION (ALSO CALLED A VIGIL OR WAKE)—Time set aside for friends and family to gather at the funeral home to pay respects to the person who has died and to offer condolences to the immediate family. The time and place of the "visitation" (also called visiting hours) should be included in the obituary.

WAKE (This definition was handed down by the author's Irish grandmother)— In times past when visitations were held in homes, mourners would gather around the deceased and share stories and toast him/her with drinks. The gatherings were loud and boisterous with the intention to "wake" the dead. "Surely he or she would wake and join the party if not truly dead."

A Memorial for My Loved One

When someone we love passes away we often experience a flood of memories of how that person touched our lives and the lives of other family members, the community, and the world. Today we may feel as if we will never forget this loved one. However, as time passes our memories do fade. This 'Memorial' section is provided help you to record those special memories and to create a permanent remembrance that will bring joy and comfort to you, and perhaps other family members, when you want to remember your loved one in the days and years to come.

My Friend/Family Member

The name of the person who has passed away is:

> ✌ *His/her date and place of birth is:*

> ✌ *His/her date and place of death is:*

How did you know or how were you related to this person?

How did your loved one pass away?

Where and what type of services were held for your loved one?

Describe your loved one who passed away

What did he/she look like? (Include things like color of hair, color of eyes, smile, birthmarks, tall or short, skinny or fat, and anything that uniquely describes the person.)

What types of clothes did he/she like to wear?

What facial expressions did this person often use? (If you cannot describe it, draw a picture!)

What did your loved one like to do for fun?

What did he/she do for work?

List and describe his/her family.

About My Loved One and Me

Write down the things the two of you would talk about together.

   ✖   *What was the last thing you talked about?*

Write down the things the two of you would do together.

✖   *What was the last thing you did together?*

Write down some of the things your loved one did for you.

✖   *What was the last thing he/she did for you?*

Write down some of the things you did for this person.

✖   *What was the last thing you did for him/her?*

Some of my loved one's favorite things

What were some of his/her favorites? If you don't know, write down what you think were his/her favorites and explain why.

Animal:

Beverage:

Bible verse or story:

Book:

Color:

Exercise:

Food:

Hobby:

Holiday:

Joke:

Movie:

Place to eat:

Place to have fun:

Place to read:

Place to sit:

Place to talk on the phone:

Place to visit:

Prayer:

Saying:

Other:

Just Remembering My Loved One

Use the following pages to insert pictures of your loved one and to create a special memory of him/her. Here are some suggestions on how to use these blank pages.

1. If you had only one thing or object by which you could remember this person, what would it be? Write a story about this thing or object and/or draw a picture of it.

2. Write a letter to God and tell Him all about your loved one.

3. Write a letter to your loved one and tell him/her what you miss the most about him or her.

4. Record the story of how you met and how you became friends.

5. Create a diary and record your feelings and thoughts about your loved one and his/her death. You may even want to keep a record of your feelings on a daily basis for a while. See how much you can remember and record in a year!